On Purpose

Principles to Help You Live
Intentionally and Grow Exponentially

Estreanda Yates

renownpublishing

Renown Publishing
www.renownpublishing.com

On Purpose / Estreanda Yates
ISBN-13: 978-1-960236-11-1

To my wonderful husband, my gifted and charming children (Braven, Titan, and Zaniya), to my brave mother, my hard-working father, my sweet aunt, and my loving brother—your unwavering love is the thread that holds together every chapter of this book.
I love you with all of my heart.

CONTENTS

Start Your Journey

Have you ever considered that the one thing you're most afraid to do could be the one thing you were designed to do? When I began my journey of pressing through fear, I thought that it would be about being bold and audacious, daring to be great, and living an extraordinary life. While those are certainly benefits of overcoming fear, I soon realized that there were many other treasures to discover.

My journey has involved digging deep, searching my soul, asking myself the hard questions, and constantly—I do mean constantly—stepping out of my comfort zone and choosing to do the things that intimidate me but I know God is calling me to do. I had to recognize that I was consistently allowing certain factors in my life to hold me back.

For instance, the fear of failure and the fear of rejection had a grip on me. I had so many debilitating insecurities—you know, those nagging thoughts that remind you of everything you're not. I struggled with comparison. I knew that God had given me a gift and a desire to encourage and teach other women, but I convinced myself that there wasn't any room for me as a communicator of God's Word. Other teachers of God's Word seemed like they were far more qualified than I was.

So I, like many others, became discouraged, and I disqualified myself. I took the vision and the gifting I strongly believed God had given me, and I put them on a shelf. There they sat, gathering dust, as the days went by. Ten years passed in the blink of an eye, and I realized that I wasn't any closer to that dream than when I had first received it.

I hadn't taken any consistent steps to pursue my dream and the calling God had placed on my life. The gifting God had given me and my pursuit of it had been drowned out by the demands of life. I filled my days with tasks that were urgent, necessary, or even fun, but they had nothing to do with the hidden passion God had placed in my heart. Does that sound familiar?

While those same fears still creep in today, I am now more self-aware. I am constantly working toward managing my fears and taking the actions I am responsible for taking. I am a work in progress, and I am sharing my progress so that you, too, can move toward your dreams and begin to live out the burning passion in your heart. I have not yet arrived. I am still on this journey, and I am bringing others with me.

You are more powerful than your fears.

Don't allow your fears to hold you back. Your fears don't have to control you. Instead, you can control your fears when you commit to embarking on a journey of embracing your purpose.

Learning to Live with P.U.R.P.O.S.E.

Through my experiences on my own journey, I came up with an approach to living, principles for pursuing the dreams God has placed in my heart, and now I want to share that approach with you. I call it *living with P.U.R.P.O.S.E.* These seven points are valuable principles you can revisit at any time to discover where you need to grow.

P.U.R.P.O.S.E. stands for:

P: Pursue God
U: Understand That You Are Chosen
R: Rest in the Storm
P: Pick Up Your Bed and Walk
O: Overcome the Obstacles
S: Serve Well
E: Enlist a Dream Team

Each concept in the acronym has its own dedicated chapter that explains the principle in detail and how you can take practical steps to apply it to your own life. By the end of this book, you will have a blueprint for pursuing your own God-given dreams and the confidence to start moving toward your goals. This path to P.U.R.P.O.S.E. is an ongoing journey, and the points in each chapter can be instrumental at any moment of your life. I hope that you don't pick up this book once and then return it to the shelf. I hope that you return to it over and over again and find these principles useful every time.

This Is a Journey, Not a Destination

This book is both a chronicle of my continuing journey and an opportunity for you to begin your own journey. To that end, I encourage you to pause and reflect as you read and think about what you're learning. Because this is such an important part of the process, I have incorporated questions throughout each chapter to help you more thoroughly digest the information I am sharing with you.

If you're anything like me, you tend to read books with the goal of getting to the next chapter. I know it's hard, but resist that temptation! My goal isn't simply to give you a bunch of information, but rather to empower you by helping you to cultivate a way of thinking that will enable you to find purpose in every area and season of your life.

The only way to live your life on purpose is to find and get to know the God who is *your* God, the God who has been fighting to be your God since the beginning of time. He is a personal God, and as you seek Him, He will speak to you in personal and profound ways. The questions in this book will help you to peel back the layers that have grown over your heart so you can hear Jesus speaking to you personally.

The biggest challenge with finding purpose is that most people never really take the time to seek it. We tend to focus on arriving at an end goal, such as a particular job, role, position, or status. My challenge to you is to see purpose as something you discover continually as you journey with Jesus. You can get rid of the belief that purpose will fall into your lap, and you can stop waiting for someone else to tell you what your purpose in life is.

It's up to *you* to start your journey. Living on purpose happens when you are intentional, and you commit to the process. No matter where you are today, you can begin living your life on purpose, and this book will give you encouragement along the way.

Thankfully, we are not called to undertake the pursuit of purpose alone. God has given us His guidance, and He has given us other people. The pursuit of purpose is lifelong and continually unfolding. Wherever you may be right now, it's not too late to begin.

You picked up this book for a reason. You are ready for change. You have been waiting on the sidelines for far too long. You know that there's something more to this life, and you're ready to experience it. It's time to rise up and live wholeheartedly!

Think of me as the coach in your corner. I am committed to helping you take the steps that will move you from fear to freedom and lead you to live more courageously. You are only one decision away from your whole life changing. So turn that page, and let's get started!

CHAPTER ONE

Laying a Strong Foundation

*Anyone who listens to my teaching and follows it
is wise, like a person who builds a house on solid
rock.*

— *Jesus (Matthew 7:24 NLT)*

Before a race begins, the official in charge says,
"Runners, to your marks!" A runner's mark is the position
from which he or she begins a race. In order to run their
best race, runners need to have a strong foundation. Can
you imagine if they showed up to the race without having
trained or prepared?

As the coach in your corner, I want to set you up for
success. I want to position you to run your best race ever.
Before we explore the seven principles of living with
P.U.R.P.O.S.E., I want to help you lay down a strong
foundation.

During my years as a college athlete, my coach was a
world-class trainer who had worked with some of the very
best. His strategy was to elevate the beliefs and
perspectives of his athletes. He challenged our way of

thinking, transforming us not only as athletes, but also as individuals. That's what I want to do for you.

With athletic training, the process is more important than the goal. Shortcuts like steroids may get athletes to their goals more quickly, but they end up sacrificing their long-term health and missing out on the opportunity to build genuine strength and stamina. Without the right process, achieving a goal becomes hollow and insincere.

Likewise, I could easily give you a formula for living on P.U.R.P.O.S.E. and tell you to go and apply it, but that wouldn't empower you to run well. Instead of relying on a one-size-fits-all formula, you will learn how to think for yourself and apply a set of principles to the specific situations in your own life.

Foundational Step #1:
Receive Direction from God

When Jesus was on earth and sought His Father in prayer, He received direction and purpose. We see this time and time again in Scripture. As a matter of fact, the Bible says He often withdrew to lonely places and prayed. If Jesus Himself met with God often, He must have known His need for consistent connection and direction. Jesus knew the recipe to experiencing God fully.

Jesus prayed during His baptism (Luke 3:21 NIV). He prayed before He started His ministry. He prayed before choosing His twelve disciples (Luke 6:12 NIV). He prayed before performing miracles (Luke 22:19). He prayed when He knew He was being led to the cross, and He prayed while He was being beaten on the cross (Luke 22:40–44, Luke 23:46).

I have seen the power of seeking God in my own life when I have sought Him for direction. When I seek the Lord, He comes through for me in astounding ways. God has shown me the pathway to peace when my heart has been troubled. He's given me vision and clarity when I have felt lost and overwhelmed. When I have sought God, I've been blessed to hear His audible voice.

When I served in the homeless ministry and really wanted to take the right steps to move the ministry forward, I went on a prayer walk at Mission Bay to seek God for direction. I felt I heard God telling me to start a fitness bootcamp that would raise money for the homeless ministry I was leading. I had run track for San Diego State University, and little did I know, God eventually would use my gifts and talents to raise money for the homeless. But, I still didn't know what exactly to do or how to do it.

I don't often ask God for a sign, but in this case, I did. I prayed to the Lord and asked Him if He would show me a sign that this was something He'd want me to do. I sat alongside the beautiful blue bay, journaling and praying in my heart. After I finished journaling, I gathered my things and walked to my car.

On my way to the car, two ladies walked over to me, introduced themselves, and said, "We sense the Lord asking us to pray for you for direction. Can we pray for you?"

I remember the shock on my face. My jaw dropped. I had just asked God for a sign. I had just sought Him in prayer for direction, and I wholeheartedly believe He used two "random" women to speak powerful words over me. The Lord had given me the sign I needed to move forward.

A few days later, a gym happened to be closing, and I was able to get some friends to help me pick up workout equipment. When the gym management found out what I was doing, they donated the equipment to me. My church opened the doors for me to recruit our church members for the bootcamp after service. We had over one hundred participants in that camp. I raised over $50,000 for the homeless ministry, and so many people were blessed!

In Psalm 34:4 the Psalmist says, "I sought the Lord, and he answered me. He delivered me from all my fears." This verse sums up my journey of walking through my fears and living *on purpose*. I want the same thing for you. Jesus wants the same thing for you, too. His word says that He will guide us to the best pathway for lives (Psalm 32:8). He wants you to seek Him and know Him as the one who can direct your life. He wants to free you from your fears, bring you closer to His heart, and give you a life of abundance. He's ready to answer prayers you didn't even know existed. Since before time began, He's always had a plan for you, and He has always wanted you to live with purpose, on purpose!

To move forward with purposeful and intentional living, we need to prioritize receiving direction from God. As we spend more time with God, we will learn to hear Him speaking into our lives. In Mark 1:38–39, Jesus left His time of prayer with clear direction. He told His disciples, "Let us go somewhere else—to the nearby villages—so I can preach there also. That is why I have come" (NIV). He knew He had to leave where He was and fulfill the mission His Father had given Him. He knew which direction to go and what His assignment was when He got there. Now that's living *on purpose*!

However, God doesn't always give us the specifics we would like, which tends to create the following responses in us:

- We find ourselves paralyzed.

- We fear what other people will think.

- We fear failure.

- Our insecurities start to surface.

Jesus came out of His time of prayer knowing the reason He had come: to preach. When God gives you one thing to do, focus on doing that one thing. I tend to get caught up in wanting other things. Being a Martha—who I will discuss more later—I start focusing on these other things because I believe that they will somehow get me to my desired destination sooner, or I simply distract myself with busy tasks. All the while, God wants me to focus on accomplishing one thing, not a thousand and one things. Yes, Jesus did other things besides preaching, but He was clear on the primary task His Father had given Him.

As I have spent more time with God and personally stepped out in faith, I have gained clarity about what I should be focusing on. I love working on the administrative side of things as well as organizing events and big projects. While I am good at those things, I have learned that God has called me to use my teaching gifts, so that's what I focus on whenever I have the opportunity.

Question: What are some of the things you do well?

_____

_____

_____

_____

_____

_____

Question: Now it's time to be honest with yourself. Is there a task God has given you that you're not pursuing? Or is there a gift He has called you to use that you have put aside? If so, what excuses are you making for why you're not using that gift or focusing on that task?

_____

_____

_____

_____

_____

_____

Question: What message has God spoken to your heart that you have forgotten or neglected? Have you busied yourself with the daily tasks of life and allowed them to drown out something you really feel called to do?

_____

_____

_____

_____

_____

_____

Jesus healed the sick, cast out demons, and raised people from the dead, but He made it clear that He came to preach. Though He was capable of doing all kinds of things, His primary focus was preaching the gospel of God's kingdom. Just as with Jesus, it's essential that we know the main purpose to which God has called us and how He will be most glorified in our lives. You can fill your time doing things that you're good at, or you can fill your time doing things that fulfill the purpose for which you believe God created you, things that only you can do in the distinct ways you do them.

Question: Think about the tasks you spend time doing regularly. Are you doing the tasks that you're designed to do, or do you spend most of your time on things that you can do well but were not ultimately created to do?

_____

_____

_____

_____

_____

_____

Foundational Step #2: Count the Cost

The next thing we need to do to establish a strong foundation for our journey is learn how to count the cost of living in response to the significance and purpose God reveals to us. Far too often, we miss out on what life has to offer us because we think that the sacrifices we'll have to make and the risks we'll have to take to reach our goal outweigh the goal itself. We need to keep the big picture in mind.

In Luke 14:25–27 (NIV), Jesus told the people what it would cost them to follow Him:

> *Large crowds were traveling with Jesus, and turning to them he said: "If anyone comes to me and does not hate father and mother, wife and children, brothers and sisters—yes, even their own life—such a person cannot be my disciple. And whoever does not carry their cross and follow me cannot be my disciple."*

Jesus was clear about what following Him would cost His disciples. It's important to understand that in the context of these verses, the word *hate* means to love less by comparison.[1] To follow Jesus, we must make Him our priority, our foremost love. We must love Him more than everyone and everything else. This can be a tough pill to swallow, but Jesus said that there is no other way.

In Luke 14:28–30 (NIV), Jesus further explained the necessity of counting the cost of following Him:

> *Suppose one of you wants to build a tower. Won't you first sit down and estimate the cost to see if you have enough money to complete it? For if you lay the foundation and are not able to finish it, everyone who sees it will ridicule you, saying, "This person began to build and wasn't able to finish."*

In other words, before we spring into action, we need to sit and consider what it will take to get us to our desired outcome and whether we are willing to surrender the things that are holding us back.

Letting Go of Expectations

I have walked through many challenges on my journey of learning to live on purpose and pursuing what God has placed in my heart. For example, I have a fear of rejection. I want to avoid it at all costs. However, as a speaker and writer, I put on events for women's ministries. Most of the time, my audience is lively and receptive, but sometimes I spot people in the audience who don't seem as visibly enthusiastic. Speaking to an audience that doesn't appear to be engaged requires me to sacrifice my expectations of how God will work through me.

I decided at the very beginning that my calling would not be dictated by how many women attend the event or how they respond to me. I would do what God gifted me to do with all of my heart. I would serve women by encouraging them to be who God designed them to be.

My calling requires me not only to surrender control and expectation, but also to face the risk of rejection. When I meet with pastors or church leaders to offer my services, they can say "yes," or they can say "no." As scary as rejection can be, I have to face that risk if I am going to do what God has gifted me to do.

Every single time I step out to teach, I must face my fear of rejection and set aside my expectation of how people will receive my teaching. I have to give up my desire to please people in order to serve people wholeheartedly. This takes lots of prayer and preparation. I have to feel the fear and still choose to step out of my comfort zone.

Sacrificing my expectations and risking rejection are part of what's required for me to start building and to finish it. These are not easy sacrifices to make or risks to take, but this is the cost of what I believe it looks like to follow Jesus in my life. There are instances when I get emails stating that my services are not needed, and that stings! I have to ask myself why I am willing to put myself through all this, why I want to pursue this dream, and the answer is that I want to see the passion God placed in my heart come to life. I want to live a life that isn't mundane and dreamless, but challenges me to seek Jesus and serve other people with all of my heart.

When God's dreams become a reality in my life, my husband will be blessed, my children will be blessed, I will be blessed, and the people who experience God through my life will be blessed. I know that my best life is being who God created me to be and doing what He created me to do.

Remember that the outcome is not as important as the process. It doesn't matter if I'm speaking to an arena packed with thousands of women who are eager to hear the message God has given me or if I'm speaking to half a dozen women who are not sure what to make of the message I'm delivering. What matters is that I am faithful to the process of what God has asked me to do and how He has told me to do it.

Now it's time to ask yourself what counting the cost looks like for you.

Question: Is there something God is impressing on your heart? In what way might God be calling you to serve and help others?

_____

_____

_____

_____

_____

Question: What is holding you back? Is it fear of failure? Is it fear of what other people might think of you? Are you afraid that people will reject what you commit to doing with your life? Are you distracted? What do you need to surrender to the Lord so that you can pursue the purpose you believe He has given you? What are you allowing to stop you?

_____

_____

_____

_____

_____

_____

Question: What sacrifices might you need to make and what risks might you need to take in the process of pursuing your God-given dream?

_____

_____

_____

_____

_____

Motives are important to God (James 4:3). If your passion honors God, go for it! Stop procrastinating and asking God whether it's really from Him. If it isn't from Him, don't worry; He will redirect your path. Don't sit on an idea that could be not only a good idea, but a God idea, because you're afraid or waiting for a sign.

Question: Now that you have taken the time to think about what you want, ask yourself why you want it. Be real and raw with yourself and with Jesus.

_____

_____

_____

_____

_____

_____

It's easy to start something; it's much harder to stick with it. I believe that's why Jesus asked for the ultimate commitment up front.

A wise builder understands the level of commitment required to finish the task.

The more something costs, the greater value we tend to place on it. Your dream may be God's dream for you, and it may require everything you have in you.

Foundational Step #3: Check Your Order

As you seek to live on purpose, it's essential to *check your order*. You need to evaluate your priorities and regularly ask yourself, *"Are my priorities in order?"* If you want the best life possible, the life God has for you, you must be willing to make Jesus your priority, your foremost love. Don't be so committed to your dreams and passions that you prioritize them above your relationship with Jesus and fail to listen to His voice.

> *Your best life requires Jesus to be first.*
> *When He is first, your life and your*
> *passions will move in the right direction.*

In my own life, when I check my order, I can clearly sense when my priorities are out of line. When I am not at my peak, I am more judgmental and critical, and my attitude stinks. I can tell when I haven't made time to bring Jesus into every space in which I find myself. When I am not thriving in my attitude and actions, I have to ask myself, *"Am I prioritizing Jesus? Am I clinging to the power of prayer and conversing with Jesus when I need direction, clarity, and an overall better attitude?"*

I am such a goal-oriented person that I can easily become fixated on my to-do list. I end up frantically attempting to get through my day, too busy to sit with Jesus and too distracted to bring Him mindfully into every aspect of my life. It's so important to pause and take a look at your relationship with Jesus, your dreams, your family, your friends, and the relationship you have with yourself. Consider how you spend your time and what motivates your choices. Then ask yourself what you are prioritizing over Jesus.

When we become frantic and overwhelmed in our day-to-day lives, we need to check our order. In my home, we try to make our priorities God, family, friends, and service, followed by everything else. Take a moment to reflect on the order of your priorities.

Question: Consider the season of life you're in right now. What are three to five things that are most important to you?

_____

_____

_____

_____

_____

Question: Have you prioritized these things over your relationship with Jesus?

_____

_____

_____

_____

_____

When you start something new or leave something behind and when you plan your schedule, it's imperative to have your priorities in place and know what tasks those priorities require. Not only do priorities help us to plan ahead, but they also help us to make wise decisions right now.

I make sure to evaluate my priorities when I'm planning out my week. God is my first priority, so I ask myself, *"How much time am I devoting to praying and studying my Bible?"* I literally carve out time to spend with God on my schedule or to-do list. Family is my second priority, so I schedule time to give to my family. I plan the activities we'll do on the weekend and what dinners we'll eat together.

Ministry is another priority. Looking at the week ahead, I ask myself, *"What meetings should I plan to have to further my dream of ministering to other women, and what meetings will take away from the priorities I have in place? What is the one thing I really want to accomplish each day to move me closer to my dream?"* As a wife and mother, I share my priorities and plans with my spouse so that we're on the same page and know how to support each other during the week. Not all weeks go as planned, but all weeks are planned with my priorities in place.

Prioritizing without a plan to execute can be futile. Deciding what your priorities are will help you to stay on track. Planning your day, week, and month with your priorities at the forefront of your mind will help you to stay intentional. Following through on your plan will help you to get results. When you plan your week, prioritize your priorities.

Question: Take some time to think about the top priorities you listed. What practical step(s) can you take today to start living according to your priorities?

_____

_____

_____

_____

_____

_____

Foundational Step #4:
Be Obedient to What God Tells You

Ten years ago, the Lord placed a calling on my heart to teach His Word, but I was scared to pursue the vision He had given me. I ran a ministry at the time, and whenever I had an opportunity to teach or speak to a group, I delegated it to other people because I was fearful. I was afraid of what other people might think of me and the rejection I might feel if I didn't do a good job of explaining the gospel message.

But then the things I once loved, the things I was good at doing, such as organizing people and projects, became burdensome and mundane. I wanted more from God, and I knew in my heart that He had more for me. I kept asking Him in prayer to show me what He wanted me to do. I knew that I wasn't truly living the life God had for me. I was made for more.

One morning, after a fairly ordinary time of journaling, prayer, and Bible study, I got out my cleaning supplies and settled into my task of cleaning the house. While I was scrubbing away, I heard the Lord say to me, *"What is the one thing I told you to do?"* At that moment, I realized that God was telling me to equip others. He was telling me to teach.

I now had a focus, but I didn't know exactly what to do or where to start. I went to the women's ministry leader at the church I was attending and asked if there were any opportunities available to equip women. That opened the door for me to teach an eight-week course, which evolved into this book.

What's beautiful is that my God-given gift for organizing people and activities complements my God-given purpose of teaching women. I get to organize the manner in which I equip and encourage women to walk in their gifts. I love it!

Sometimes God calls us to something big, and we feel so overwhelmed that we become paralyzed. We feel stuck and unable to move forward. I want to encourage you with the words that my pastor, George Clerie, spoke over me when I didn't know where to begin with all of my ideas and lack of knowledge: "Start with what you know." If you focus on what you don't know, you'll never be able to move forward. If you focus on what you do know, you'll often realize that it's enough to get started.

Sometimes we're hungry for God to call us to do something big, but He may be calling us to be faithful in the little things. Let's not minimize the power of serving in small or behind-the-scenes roles. In this case, living On Purpose may mean staying faithful in something and not abandoning it when it becomes difficult or inconvenient.

Sometimes living On Purpose means getting rid of the things in our lives that are causing us harm, such as lust, unforgiveness, shame, and guilt. You may need to seek help to overcome an addiction, or you may need counseling to work through trauma you have experienced. Whatever it is, go for it!

If you don't know where to start, start with where you are and what you know.

I didn't know much about writing a book or what the full process of creating a book would require. I started with my laptop, a blank piece of paper, and ideas. I started with what I knew how to do, and I *kept doing* what I knew how to do.

Question: What's one concrete thing you can do to start pursuing what God has called you to do? Chances are that this first step will take you out of your comfort zone. Say "yes" anyway!

_____

_____

_____

_____

_____

_____

One concrete thing I did to pursue God's calling for me was to set up the meeting with the women's ministry leader. Doing this was scary, but it allowed God to enter into my fears and teach me what it means to press through those fears with Him. Since then, every step I have taken in obedience has launched me out of my comfort zone and landed me in a place where I have found a greater depth of intimacy with Jesus.

People knew me as an organizer, not a teacher, so I took on that title and identity instead of pursuing my God-given passions. I allowed other people's limited experience and knowledge of me, as well as my own fears, to dictate my actions. People would ask me to complete administrative tasks because they didn't see me as a teacher, and I was afraid to tell them that I believed God was calling me to something else, so I stayed in the administration box.

Sometimes we're so afraid to be who we are that we shrink back and accept a mediocre existence, but God wants to do much more than we can dream to ask for. If you're waiting for someone to give you the green light, here it is, friend! Step out of the box. No one can limit you except you. I'll leave you with these two words: *you can.*

Question: Are you staying in a particular box because you're afraid that people will reject you if you do something different? How has your comfort zone or other people's opinions of where you belong kept you from pursuing God's calling?

_____

_____

_____

_____

_____

_____

Even when we hear God calling us into new territory, we may still feel stuck. We may find ourselves in a place where we lack experience and need direction from someone with more knowledge in that area. We may get distracted by a desire to figure out how all of the details will come together, or we may try to focus on too many things at one time and end up doing nothing at all. We may end up with a whole bunch of unfinished projects and little motivation to keep going. Sometimes God tells us to focus on one thing, and we need to be obedient to that.

I am the type of person who wants to believe that I can focus on fifty different things at once, but in reality, I am at my best when I'm focusing on doing a small number of things thoroughly. When I first decided to follow God's calling to something more, the one thing He placed in my heart was to teach, and I had to do my part to find an opportunity. When I was obedient to what God called me to focus on, I was met with an open door. I am so thankful that the Lord told me to focus on one thing, because when I acted on it, it was the one thing that launched me to living my life *with* purpose *on* purpose.

Question: Has God spoken to you about taking a specific action on something, but you haven't done anything because He hasn't given you clear instructions or all of the details? If so, what is it?

_____

_____

_____

_____

_____

_____

Foundational Step #5:
Commit to Being Committed

Commitment is the last step in laying a strong foundation for the process of pursuing our God-given dreams. *Commitment* can be a scary word in today's culture. I tend to associate it with restriction and a lack of freedom. But as much as I struggle with that word, commitment has added so much value to my life.

For example, writing this book took more effort and time than I could have imagined. It took everything I had in me. Instead of hanging out with my friends, spending time on social media, or getting extra sleep, I chose to invest that time in writing this book. I repeatedly got discouraged, and with a newborn baby, I certainly wanted to sleep. But each time I started to lose my resolve, I chose to recommit. I devoted my energy to writing, studying, praying, and focusing on the work in front of me rather than other things I wanted to do instead.

Writing this book also took resources. My family and I were living on one income at the time, and we knew that we would incur some costs in writing, publishing, and marketing this book. However, at the end of the day, I knew that God had placed the writing of this book on my heart, and I just had to be faithful.

If we want to be disciples of Jesus and we want our lives to look like His, we need to understand how much God values commitment. He designed commitment, and He demonstrates it better than anyone else does.

In today's culture, we tend to avoid commitment. We desire freedom, flexibility, and options, and we have convinced ourselves that we will lose those things if we commit to something. If we do begin something and it doesn't meet our expectations, we may give up and look for the next best thing.

We need a renewed, biblical perspective on commitment. Starting something is a lot easier than sticking with something. Sticking with something builds character, which goes hand in hand with commitment.

There are things in life you will never achieve without commitment, and there are things in life you will never keep without character.

God is always speaking to us, challenging us, and encouraging us. It's your relationship with Jesus that will launch you into your calling. The question is: Are you committed to following Him? Committing to Jesus is not a personal loss; it's an eternal gain!

Perhaps you need to commit or recommit to following Jesus. You can invite Him into your life with a simple prayer: "Jesus, I want to follow You. I accept You as my Lord and Savior. Please come into every aspect of my life."

Question: Let's dream for a bit about your ideal life walking with Jesus. What would it look like for you to commit or recommit to following Jesus and pursuing all that He places in your heart?

_____

_____

_____

_____

_____

If you don't know the answer to the question above, spend some time in prayer, asking God to show you. Whatever life God is calling you to live will require commitment. It will take time, effort, and resources, but God will enable you to see it through to the finish line if you stay committed. When commitment is difficult for you, ask Jesus to give you the stamina to stick with it. Then renew your commitment and keep going!

Break It Down

What do you need to commit to doing? What have you been desiring to do but haven't put the time, effort, or resources into accomplishing?

Maybe you want to get up early to spend time with God, but you haven't because that would require you to sacrifice sleep.

Maybe you want to have a healthier lifestyle so you can feel better about what you see in the mirror, have more confidence about your image, and keep up with your kids as they get older and stronger, but you haven't taken the time to plan a workout routine or prepare healthy meals.

Maybe you sense God calling you to start a business or a new ministry, but you feel overwhelmed and paralyzed when you consider the resources you believe you lack, the failure you could experience, the risks you would need to take, and the rejection you might have to face.

Living on purpose won't happen by accident. You have to be intentional. This is why it's important to have measurable goals along the way to your overall goal. If you break your big goal into manageable pieces, those smaller goals will help you to get to your big goal without being overwhelmed.

For example, if getting up early to spend time with God is too much to do all at once, try getting up five minutes earlier each day until you're able to get up half an hour early. Try working out once a week and then adding days until you have built up to a regular workout regimen. Take the time to break down the costs of that ministry or business endeavor. Then talk to one person about one aspect for which you need funding.

If looking at the big picture overwhelms you, stop looking at the big picture and just take one step at a time. Identify one task that you can do today or tomorrow and then do it! In the words of Marie Forleo, "Everything is figureoutable."[2] You were designed to climb mountains, and you are capable of meeting your goals when you intentionally commit to them.

Now I want you to put everything you have learned into one place:

```
┌─────────────────────────────────────────────────────┐
│                                                       │
│        One thing God has been telling you to do:      │
│                                                       │
│   ─────────────────────────────────────────────      │
│                                                       │
└─────────────────────────────────────────────────────┘
                          │
┌─────────────────────────────────────────────────────┐
│                                                       │
│            What's the one step you can take?          │
│                                                       │
│   ─────────────────────────────────────────────      │
│                                                       │
└─────────────────────────────────────────────────────┘
                          │
┌─────────────────────────────────────────────────────┐
│                                                       │
│   List someone you can reach out to that has          │
│   experience in the things God is calling you to do:  │
│                                                       │
│   ─────────────────────────────────────────────      │
│                                                       │
└─────────────────────────────────────────────────────┘
```

This chart will help you to see the one thing God is calling you to do, the action step you need to take to move in that direction, and a person with more experience in that area to whom you can reach out. If you're still trying to figure out your "one thing," connecting with someone who has experience you lack may help you to define what you can start doing to make progress. Remember that establishing small, measurable goals will help you to remain committed and focused.

Sometimes we really want to move forward, but we're not sure how. We get stuck trying to figure everything out. Take it from me: if you try to figure everything out before you get started, you'll never get started. Get out of your head and take action! If not, you'll look up and realize that a whole year or a whole decade has passed and no movement toward your dreams has happened. If you want different results, you need to do something different.

Setting a measurable goal and immediately completing at least one action item is the first step.

Get Set! Go!

In this chapter, we have explored the five steps to building a strong foundation that will enable you to live your life with P.U.R.P.O.S.E.:

1. Foundational Step #1: Receive Direction from God

2. Foundational Step #2: Count the Cost

3. Foundational Step #3: Check Your Order

4. Foundational Step #4: Be Obedient to What God Tells You

5. Foundational Step #5: Commit to Being Committed

Now that you have a strong foundation, you should be able to move confidently toward your God-given dreams without any hindrances, right? Not just yet. There is still one major roadblock that can prevent you from living the best life God has for you. Get set because that's where we're headed next!

Chapter One Notes
*Take some time to unpack all
your takeaways from this chapter*

_____

_____

_____

_____

_____

_____

_____

_____

_____

_____

_____

_____

_____

_____

_____

_____

_____

Fear—the Ultimate Roadblock

Courage isn't an absence of fear. It's doing what you are afraid to do. It's having the power to let go of the familiar and forge ahead into new territory.[3]
—John Maxwell

We cannot change what we do not know or cannot see. This chapter will help you to understand what fear is and identify its roots in your life so that you can start living your life on P.U.R.P.O.S.E.

Having a strong foundation doesn't matter if we allow fear to keep us from pursuing our God-given dreams.

I used to assume that fear was a negative emotion until I realized that God designed us to experience fear. In school, I learned how fear is a protective mechanism in the brain that helps us to make decisions that will keep us safe. God calls us to stay away from things that will harm us, but He doesn't intend for fear to keep us from the life He has designed for us in accordance with His promises.

What Do You Believe About Fear?

We tend to form beliefs based on our life experiences. Something happens to us, and it shapes our perspective, which affects our decisions as we move forward. Although these beliefs may be true for us according to what we have experienced in the past, it doesn't mean that they are true in light of Scripture.

We often don't take the time to examine what we believe and why we believe it. This type of reflection is essential for purposeful living because what we believe dictates our actions. Your life is a result of your choices, and your choices reflect your love and your fears.

Take your time as you answer the following questions. Peel back some layers and get real with yourself. This journey is all about doing the work!

Question: What dream has God given you? (You can use the same one you wrote down in Chapter One.)

_____

_____

_____

_____

_____

_____

Question: What are some of your fears about acting on this dream?

_____

_____

_____

_____

_____

Question: We tend to fear what other people may think about us and how they perceive us. Whose opinion about your dream frightens you the most?

_____

_____

_____

_____

_____

Question: When you think about the word fear, what are the first things that come to mind?

_____

_____

_____

_____

_____

_____

Take a moment to look at your answers. Underline what is in your control and strike out what is not in your control. You may find that the things you are afraid of tend to be the things you cannot control.

Take a hard look at your beliefs. If you suspect that any of them are not based on biblical truth, highlight them. You may find that you have been carrying around some false beliefs.

Taking on New Beliefs About Fear

To replace our false beliefs about fear with the truth of Scripture, we need to know what God's Word says about fear. Take a moment to examine the following verses:

- "The fear of the LORD is the beginning of wisdom, and knowledge of the Holy One is understanding" (Proverbs 9:10 NIV).

- "There is no fear of God before their eyes" (Romans 3:18 NIV).

- "There is no fear in love; but perfect love casts out fear, because fear involves torment. But he who fears has not been made perfect in love" (1 John 4:18 NKJV).

- "For God has not given us a spirit of fear, but of power and of love and of a sound mind" (2 Timothy 1:7 NKJV).

Notice that Scripture describes two different types of fear: the fear of the Lord and the spirit of fear. God has given us the ability to experience fear, but He has not given us a spirit of fear.

The Spirit of Fear

The spirit of fear comes in many forms: pride, laziness, procrastination, excuses, confusion, comfort, timidity, and indecisiveness. The spirit of fear is often rooted in childhood experiences. If you are struggling with fear, I encourage you to seek counseling or talk with a professional who can help you to work through your fears.

The spirit of fear is a stronghold, and God is the One who frees us from strongholds.

Let's take another look at 1 John 4:18 (NKJV) to see how God frees us from the spirit of fear:

There is no fear in love; but perfect love casts out fear, because fear involves torment. But he who fears has not been made perfect in love.

God does not torment His children. The spirit of fear encourages us to torment ourselves by imagining outcomes that will most likely never come to pass. An article on the Bible in One Year app describes fear as "overestimating the danger and underestimating [our] ability to cope."[4]

God frees us from the spirit of fear through His perfect love. Because He loves us perfectly, we can trust Him to have our best interest in mind and to control the things we cannot control. We don't have to fear the unknown or the uncontrollable, because our loving God knows everything and is in control of everything.

The Fear of the Lord

The second type of fear described in Scripture is the fear of the Lord. Fearing God means respecting Him and having a reverent attitude toward Him. As we read above, "The fear of the LORD is the beginning of wisdom, and knowledge of the Holy One is understanding" (Proverbs 9:10 NIV). This means that our fear of God—our respect for Him and reverence toward Him—is rooted in our understanding that He is who He says He is.

God is the Creator of the universe. He has power over all things and authority over heaven and hell. Fearing God means believing that He is sovereign. He has created all things, and He governs all things (Colossians 1:16–17).

Everything God has put in this world has a distinct purpose. He chose to make man in His image (Genesis 1:26)—not that we would be equal to Him, but that we would be a reflection of Him. He has given us authority over the rest of His creation. Again, God has given a purpose to everything He created. It's up to us to use our God-given intelligence to seek and find the purpose for which He created us.

The fear of the Lord is essential to pursuing our God-given dreams and the passions He places in our hearts. Let's take some time to explore what it means to fear God.

Question: Fearing God means respecting Him. Think about respect for a moment. What does it mean to respect someone?

_____

_____

_____

_____

_____

_____

When we consider how we respect those around us, such as people of high status, our bosses, pastors, and even friends, we may think of respect in terms of putting on our best behavior. We are careful to show only what we want them to see, and we reserve the parts of us that we don't want them to know about.

Respecting God doesn't look exactly like respecting people, because with Him we don't have to put on our best behavior or work hard to show Him only the strongest parts of us. We need to come to Him as we are and place in His hands the things that weigh heavily on our hearts. Respecting God does not require us to hide parts of ourselves. In fact, it's just the opposite: respecting God means coming to Him, knowing that He is our heavenly Father. We can come to Him with assurance because of who He is *to us* and with trepidation because He controls everything *for us*.

Fearing God means listening to His voice and following it. It means obeying Him and praising Him in all things and all seasons. Fearing God is seeing Him for who He is, *Almighty God*, and relinquishing your heart, mind, and actions to His sovereignty.

Question: Have you ever felt that respecting God meant hiding parts of yourself from Him? Why do you think that is? How does God want you to fear Him, and what are some practical ways you can show Him respect?

_____

_____

_____

_____

_____

_____

Question: On the contrary, what are some things you might say or do that would show disrespect toward God?

_____

_____

_____

_____

_____

_____

Fearing God means respecting Him and having a physical, mental, and emotional posture that positions Him in His rightful place in your life—the utmost highest.

What Does Fearing the Lord Look Like in Your Life?

Let's go a bit deeper. Imagine that you're a kid again and your parents tell you that you have to be home by 6 p.m. every night. If you consistently come home at 7 p.m., are you showing them respect? Of course not. Your parents told you to be home at a certain time for a reason, and your blatant disregard for what they told you is disobedience.

Similarly, let's say that God whispers in your ear, *"I want you to share your creativity with the world."* If you come home from work or school each day and fritter away your time on mindless entertainment and scrolling through social media instead of doing what God has asked you to do, isn't that also disobedience?

Fearing the Lord means respecting what He says by

following through and doing what He asks of us. When He places something on our hearts, it's disobedience for us not to pursue it.

Since we have been given a purpose by God, who has created all things and has authority over all things, that should encourage us to shake off the shackles of comfort and ungodly fear and live in courageous obedience. In other words, if He placed something on your heart, go for it! *You've got this because God's got you.*

Your beginning and middle will look different from others', so don't waste time with comparisons. God may be calling you to forgive someone. Don't minimize that. Forgiving that person could very well open doors for you that you don't know exist. Or maybe God is nudging you to get help with an addiction. Whatever it is, living a life on purpose isn't one-dimensional. It isn't just about living out your passion; it encompasses your mind, body, and soul. In three words, it's *living in freedom.*

Get Set! It's Go Time!

In this chapter, we looked at how to keep a spirit of fear from getting between you and your life of P.U.R.P.O.S.E.:

1. Recognize the false beliefs you have been carrying around. Realize that the things you are afraid of are often the things you can't control.

2. Replace your false beliefs about fear with the truth of Scripture. Because God loves you perfectly, you can trust Him to have your best

interests in mind and to control the things you cannot control.

3. Fear God by having a physical, mental, and emotional posture that puts Him in His right place—the highest position—in your life. Respect what He says by following through and doing what He asks of you.

We can live in fear, or we can seek to walk in freedom.

The spirit of fear tries to keep us in bondage, but the fear of the Lord inspires and empowers us to live on P.U.R.P.O.S.E.!

Chapter Two Notes

*Take some time to unpack all
your takeaways from this chapter*

_____

_____

_____

_____

_____

_____

_____

_____

_____

_____

_____

_____

_____

_____

_____

_____

_____

Pursue God

But Jesus often withdrew to lonely places and prayed.

—Luke 5:16 (NIV)

Since the beginning of time, God has given mankind a significant purpose in His plan, yet many of us still find ourselves wondering what our purpose is. We tend to get bogged down with confusion, and we desperately seek clarity.

We're haunted by questions such as "Is this really You, God?" and "Is this where You want me to be, God?" While God does use people, sermons, and His creation to speak to us, our true confirmation and assurance come from Him. He is our inner guide. The encouragement and guidance we receive from other people along the way are meant to affirm what God is already doing and speaking to us.

> *People are our source of confirmation,*
> *not our source of revelation.*

The good news is that you have everything you need to live your life *with* purpose *on* purpose!

Some people land amidst great opportunities and are able to thrive right away. Some people instantly know what God has created them to do in this world. Then there are some of us, myself included, who need to dig a little deeper, spend time with God, and do the work of seeking and finding Him.

It's time to take the first step on our journey of living with P.U.R.P.O.S.E. The first *P* in this acronym stands for "Pursue God."

Pursue the Source and the Fruit of Your Life Will Flourish

Spending time seeking God naturally produces fruit in our lives. If we are pursuing Him, He will get us where we need to go. People tell us to find our passion, do more of what we enjoy, and hone in on our strengths. While these things are all fine and good, it's essential to be rooted in our relationship with God so that we grow spiritually and our gifts flourish supernaturally as a result of our connection to Him.

Scripture tells us that when we abide in Christ, we will bear fruit. Jesus said, "I am the vine; you are the branches. If you remain in me and I in you, you will bear much fruit; apart from me you can do nothing" (John 15:5 NIV). Often we're so focused on the fruit—dreams, passions, and answers to our prayers—that we forget to nurture our connection to the source. We long to see the desires of our hearts materialize. If we don't abide in Christ, we may still experience great things in life, but we will rob ourselves of the richest possible life we can have here on earth. Everything we truly want in life is birthed out of our relationship with Jesus.

So many people have lots of great things going for them, but their souls are starving. In our culture, we're passion-focused and driven by our dreams. We have learned to focus on our goals instead of on the One who fuels our goals and gives us perspective and direction as we pursue them.

I served in ministry for a long time, and I found myself doing a lot of things, both in ministry and outside of it, that kept me busy and productive but didn't give me the opportunity to flourish. I avoided speaking opportunities and other things that made me feel too vulnerable and uncomfortable. In my heart, I knew that God was calling me to do the very things I was afraid of doing, but I avoided anything that I saw as a chance to fail in the eyes of others. I played it safe and created a life of busyness and productivity instead of courage and purpose.

When we are not pursuing God as our source, we can easily find ourselves serving in different roles and accomplishing a variety of tasks without using the gifts and talents God has given us. We miss out on exploring and finding the hidden gifts within us if we don't listen to what God is telling us and go for it!

If we want to live fruitful lives, we need to be intentional about pursuing and staying connected to the One who plants the seeds of dreams and visions in our hearts.

God is knocking at the door of your heart and calling you by name, saying, *"Take My hand. Follow Me. I have more for you!"*

Get Comfortable with Being Uncomfortable

I want to prepare you for what you can expect as you abide in Jesus, following Him intentionally, praying continually, and studying His Word regularly. Pursuing Jesus has both mountains and valleys. It's not always comfortable.

Let me give an example. I have two family members whom I hang out with all the time, and they are very old school. In other words, technology isn't their friend. They both want to avoid it as much as possible. I'll call them Sandy and John so that I don't put their business in the street.

Sandy is far from being tech-savvy. She has a smartphone, but she has no idea how to use it, so she carries an old flip phone as a backup. Sandy has very little patience for the learning process of using her smartphone. Whenever she takes out her smartphone, I know that it will only be a matter of minutes before she shoves it back into her purse in frustration and starts digging for her flip phone.

Sandy's frustration with her new smartphone reminds me of how we tend to respond to our walk with Jesus. When we get frustrated with something new, we don't hang in there long enough to let the uncomfortable become more comfortable. Instead, we go back to the things that are already comfortable for us.

Here's the thing: truly pursuing God is not always comfortable. It requires us to be intentional and to read the instruction manual, the Bible, perhaps with a daily devotional. It requires us to allow God into our space and to call out to Him for help. When God calls us to step into something new, we need to realize that it's not going to be comfortable at first. Stick it out and give it time. Keep pushing ahead!

Now as for John, he takes a different approach to his smartphone troubles. Instead of taking the time to learn how to use his phone, he hands it to me when he gets frustrated or can't figure out how to do something. He asks me to do whatever he needs for him because he doesn't know how to do it himself.

Some of us have a similar mindset when it comes to our faith. We take the easier route that requires less effort on our part, expecting someone else to do for us what we could do for ourselves. If we would just do our part and spend time with the Creator, we would experience a richness in life that no person or thing on this earth can give us.

Nowadays, if we want to learn almost anything, we can Google or YouTube it to get visual step-by-step instructions. The information is at the tips of our fingers; we just need to seek it out. It's the same with Jesus.

*The information that your soul needs
in this lifetime is accessible to you,
and it's at your fingertips.*

Our Creator knows how to help us dig up and bring to life the beauty that's buried in us. We simply need to seek Him! When God created you, He had a vision in mind, a significant role for you to fill. God gives identity and purpose to everything He creates. He has not created anything without a purpose.

If you want to know what God created you for, you need to spend time with Him. In my life, I have found that spending time with Jesus turns my chaos into calm, my confusion into clarity, and my passions into purpose. He gives me peace in my pursuits and strength in difficult seasons.

Question: Think of a really special moment you spent or experienced with the Lord. Where were you in life and in your walk with Jesus? What was special about that moment?

_____

_____

_____

_____

_____

_____

Question: What is one thing you can do to create more opportunities to experience the Lord in that way?

_____

_____

_____

_____

_____

_____

In seasons of difficulty or discouragement, God may seem distant, or we may feel stuck because we lack wisdom or experience. Abiding in Jesus and spending time in fellowship with others, especially those who are spiritually mature in God's Word, could be the missing pieces we need to begin moving forward.

I don't want you to feel guilty or discouraged if you're not reading the Bible every day. I don't want you to feel like you won't find joy in life or purpose if you don't read the Bible. This is about you having a personal relationship with Jesus. I'm sharing what has worked for me. As I have studied and followed many other Christians whom I admire, I have found this to be a common thread in their lives as well.

It's up to you to figure out what your walk with Jesus will look like. It's up to you to ask yourself what type of relationship you truly want with Jesus and what you need to do to walk with your Creator. That's what this section is about: you walking with your Creator, your personal guide, your heavenly Father, your friend. In my journey, walking with Jesus has been everything, and I want the same for you!

Prioritize the Good Part

Let's dig a little deeper into what it looks like to pursue God in order to live with P.U.R.P.O.S.E. Luke 10:38–42 (AMP) teaches us to prioritize the right things:

Now while they were on their way, Jesus entered a village [called Bethany], and a woman named Martha welcomed Him into her home. She had a sister named Mary, who seated herself at the Lord's feet and was continually listening to His teaching. But Martha was very busy and distracted with all of her serving responsibilities; and she approached Him and said, "Lord, is it of no concern to You that my sister has left me to do the serving alone? Tell her to help me and do her part." But the Lord replied to her, "Martha, Martha, you are worried and bothered and anxious about so many things; but only one thing is necessary, for Mary has chosen the good part [that which is to her advantage], which will not be taken away from her."

Jesus wants us to welcome Him into the most vulnerable places of our lives. Martha welcomed Jesus into her home. I think of home as the place where most of our walls come down. Home is designed to be a safe place.

People and things we don't trust or we don't consider safe are not allowed into our homes.

When we choose to invite guests into our homes, we desire to embrace them and get to know them. We want to make them part of our safe haven. Martha chose to let Jesus into her home. She wanted to create the perfect experience for Him, but He simply wanted to be with her.

I love that the first thing Martha did in this passage was to welcome Jesus into her home. Let's take a moment to digest what was happening here.

> *Jesus desires to come into*
> *the home of your heart.*
> *He wants you to allow Him into*
> *the intimate spaces of your life.*

Remember that God is omniscient. He already knows about those vulnerable areas. You don't have to hide anything from Him. You can ask Jesus to come into those spaces and change them by bringing healing, renewed perspective, and peace. If you're holding back from Him in an area of your life or you think that you need to have it all together before you let Him in, ask Him to teach you how to surrender.

Question: What are some vulnerable places in your life where you have edged God out because you want everything to be perfect before you let Him in?

What areas of your life have you not truly let God into?

_____

_____

_____

_____

_____

_____

Jesus Wants You More Than Anything Else

Jesus was in Martha's home! Imagine having your favorite celebrity or political figure in your home. It would be an honor and a privilege to have that person visit, and you would probably work very hard to make sure that everything was absolutely perfect according to your standards.

From Martha's perspective, the reality of Jesus' experience in her home was falling drastically short of her expectations. She was working hard to give Him the best of the best. Jesus, on the other hand, was not looking for the same perfection Martha had in mind. He was far more interested in her soul than in her work. In fact, Jesus would have preferred that Martha stop trying to make everything perfect.

We can stop working hard to please Jesus, other people, and even ourselves.

*Jesus doesn't require you to have a
perfect home or a perfect heart.
He wants you, with all of your imperfections.*

Please don't misunderstand. It was not a bad thing that Martha was working. She invited Jesus into her home, and it was very important to her that Jesus felt welcomed. What was going on here was that Martha was prioritizing her *self-imposed* responsibilities over spending time with Jesus.

Martha was focused on making everything just right according to her standards when it was more important for her to stop and spend time with Jesus, even if that meant that things were not exactly how she wanted them to be. Scripture says that Martha felt "worried," "bothered," and "anxious" (Luke 10:41 AMP). When we focus on doing things for Jesus, people, and even our own sense of significance instead of focusing on being with Jesus, we will experience the same emotions. Sometimes we just need to stop, pause, pray, and invite God into every area of our lives. Then we can reassess our motives and prioritize what's important.

You Have the Power to Choose

To Martha, the issue was that her sister wasn't helping her to take care of the guests and Jesus wasn't telling her sister to help. Martha's self-imposed obligations gave her the impression that everyone else was the problem and it had nothing to do with her. In reality, however, Martha had the power to choose.

When we are overwhelmed, it's easy to blame other people instead of looking at our own choices and priorities.

Notice that Jesus said, "Mary has *chosen* the good part" (Luke 10:42 AMP, emphasis added). Martha was pointing fingers instead of realizing that she had the power to make a choice. We all have the power to choose. When we are frustrated with other people and overwhelmed with our self-imposed responsibilities, we need to ask ourselves, *"What choices am I making that are producing the results I am experiencing?"* We also need to take inventory of our motives and ask ourselves if our work is keeping us from feeding our souls.

Martha's desire to be hospitable to Jesus was good, but her priorities were in the wrong order. Her desire to please Jesus by doing things for Him distracted her from spending time with Him. At this moment, Martha's mindset needed to change from work to worship.

There is surely a time to work, but it would have been to Martha's advantage if, like Mary, she had left her work to sit and be with Jesus. It takes more faith to let go of our need to achieve than to hold on to it. Surrendering our goals, timelines, and the areas in which we are gifted requires trusting God.

This is not a call to forfeit responsibility. It's a reminder to prioritize what is truly important.

Question: What specific activities are distracting you from spending time with Jesus and connecting with Him?

_____

_____

_____

_____

_____

_____

Often we worry that if we don't focus on our responsibilities all of the time, things won't get done and we'll end up with a sense of failure. I truly believe that God has designed us for achievement and victory. As I have studied the Bible, I have seen the distinction in many biblical figures. As wives, we want to encourage and support our husbands. As mothers, we often feel responsible to love, teach, and nurture our children and provide a home environment that allows them to flourish. As professionals, we want to thrive in our vocations. As entrepreneurs, we want our businesses to be wildly successful.

It takes faith to believe that our soul work is more important than our responsibilities and achievements. If we commit to carving out time to take care of our souls, then the things we are responsible for have greater potential to flourish beyond what we can imagine.

Question: How does it make you feel to know that it will take faith to step away from your work routines and responsibilities to carve out time to make Jesus a priority in your life? What practical steps can you take to make that shift?

_____

_____

_____

_____

_____

_____

Know When to Step Away from Your Work

The fact that Martha said that Mary "left" her (Luke 10:40 AMP) indicates that Mary had been working with Martha but, at some point, decided to stop working and sit at the feet of Jesus.

In our daily lives, we tend to get caught up in the task at hand. Martha seems like a Type A personality, the kind of person who likes to work and get things done. That's my personality all the way! Some people consider Type A personalities to be workaholics, perfectionists, and overachievers, but I like to say that we love progress and enjoy the results we experience when our efforts materialize in the manner we hoped they would. When we prioritize our tasks over Jesus, however, our work can become burdensome. We may also become entitled and start placing unreasonable expectations on others.

We need to know when it's time to step away from the responsibilities we love and sit with the One who loves us. For some of us, this may mean not cleaning or doing the dishes right away so that we can be present with our children. It may mean turning off the cell phone so that we can unplug from the world and our work and reconnect with the ones we love. If you're a stay-at-home mom, it may mean asking your husband, a family member, or a close friend to take over child-care duties for a few hours so you can have some time to yourself or go out to spend quality time with friends.

Sitting at the feet of Jesus means that we invite Him and incorporate Him into every aspect of our lives. The more we cultivate a lifestyle of spending time with God, the more we will find that He gives us the perspective, wisdom, peace, and guidance for which our souls are thirsting.

When things are out of order, check your order! As Jesus said to Martha, prioritize "the good part" (Luke 10:42 AMP).

Question: Whom do you identify with most: Mary, who sat at the feet of Jesus, or Martha, who worked hard to make everything just right? How are their characteristics and choices reflected in your life?

_____

_____

_____

_____

_____

_____

Question: What is Jesus showing you in this Scripture passage?

_____

_____

_____

_____

_____

_____

Question: How can you apply this message to your own life?

_____

_____

_____

_____

_____

_____

Creating a Routine That Helps You Thrive

Living on purpose requires us to have daily routines that set us up for success, beginning first thing in the morning. I have noticed that one thing highly effective people have in common is their implementation of healthy routines. From entrepreneurs to pastors, people who are really thriving in their spheres of influence incorporate a regular time of solitude into their busy schedules, allowing them to clear their minds, re-energize, and refocus.

In Mark 1:35–39 (NIV), Jesus gave us the perfect example of having a morning routine that sets you up for success:

> *Very early in the morning, while it was still dark, Jesus got up, left the house and went off to a solitary place, where he prayed. Simon and his companions went to look for him, and when they found him, they exclaimed: "Everyone is looking for you!"*
>
> *Jesus replied, "Let us go somewhere else—to the nearby villages—so I can preach there also. That is why I have come." So he traveled throughout Galilee, preaching in their synagogues and driving out demons.*

People were looking for Jesus, but Jesus was looking for His heavenly Father before He began His work of the day. When you are living a life of true purpose and significance, people will seek you out because they admire what God is doing in your life. It's important that you keep your focus on God so that you can lead the people who are following you to Jesus. Living on purpose requires us to have routines that empower us to lead well.

Let's dig deeper into Jesus' example in Mark 1:35–39 so that we, too, can live with great intention as God allows our lives to impact others.

Question: Jesus woke up "very early in the morning, while it was still dark" (Mark 1:35 niv). What does that tell you about Jesus, the greatest leader who has ever walked this earth?

_____

_____

_____

_____

_____

_____

Jesus was awake early—not to farm, fish, or prepare for a day selling goods in the marketplace like other early risers in His culture, but to pray.

Spending time with God isn't some religious thing we do so that we can be good with God. In Christ, we are already good with God. There's nothing we can do to make ourselves any better in God's eyes. Jesus took care of everything on the cross.

We spend time with God so that we can know Him more intimately and live the fruitful lives He calls us to live. We stay connected with Him so we can know Him and make Him known. The more time we spend with God, the better our lives will reflect Him to others and the more fully we will experience His goodness here on earth.

Reading the Bible and spending time with God isn't for Him; it's for us. God gave up His Son so you and I could have a relationship with Him. Because of Jesus' sacrificial death on the cross for our sins, we can come boldly before God any time we want. We can open and steward this gift of access to God by spending time with Him, or we can leave it on the shelf.

That said, if you haven't been spending time with God, there's no need to beat yourself up. God isn't mad at you! Instead of beating yourself up, start learning how to open this gift on a daily basis. You can spend time with Jesus anytime and anywhere. Your time with Jesus doesn't have to look like someone else's, even if you consider that person to be a perfect Christian.

> **The perfect Christian doesn't exist,**
> **but the purposeful Christian does.**

Even if someone's social media accounts paint the portrait of a perfect Christian, it doesn't exist. My slogan is: "I love Jesus and have some of the same struggles that you have!" You are not alone.

To live on purpose, you have to be willing to spend time with God, and that means figuring out what works for you. For me, morning is the best time because it gives me motivation for my day. It's important to establish a morning routine that sets you up for success by helping you to clarify your purpose for your day and your life. Jesus gave us an example of this approach when He woke up before sunrise to spend time with His Father.

Every person whose life I have admired had a morning routine. I once heard Rachel Hollis, a motivational speaker, say in an interview, "If you own the morning, then you own the day!"[5] I believe that with all my heart. When I sacrifice sleep and wake up early in the morning to make my day intentional, I have the most productive days.

I wake up in the morning, drink something cold, read my Bible, and journal. Then I work on something I really want to get done before my world needs me—my world being my husband, my kids, and my team. I finish with a workout. If I'm having a bad morning, I may write a list of all the things I'm grateful for, or I may write out affirmations of Jesus' promises and purpose for my life.

When I don't follow this morning routine to prepare and motivate myself, I spend most of the day responding to what comes my way and fighting through the chaos to accomplish things I want to get done. By the end of the day, I'm in a bad mood because, though I was extremely busy, I wasn't able to meet my goals.

Question: Brainstorm some different ways you can create a healthy morning routine for yourself that sets you up for a successful day. It may involve reading the Bible, journaling, taking a walk or jog,

or having a cup of coffee before the responsibilities
of the day begin.

_____

_____

_____

_____

_____

_____

Creating a morning ritual in your life will help you to
clear your mind, experience God, and find peace within
your soul and the purpose in your heart. Intentionally
spending time with God on a daily basis will position you
to live a life of P.U.R.P.O.S.E.

Your time with God may feel uncomfortable at first.
You may not know what to say to Him and sitting in
silence to listen to His voice may feel awkward. Don't let
that discourage you! If you stick with it, it will change
your life.

I designed the Seven-Day Solitude Plan to help you
start spending time with God in His Word. Over the next
seven days, this tool will teach you to meditate on the
Word of God. It incorporates several different approaches
so you can develop your own unique routine of spending
personal time with Jesus.

Get Set! Go!

In this chapter, we learned that living with P.U.R.P.O.S.E. happens when you pursue God:

1. Instead of focusing on your goals first, focus on God as your source. Let Him be the One who fuels your goals and gives you perspective and direction. Trust Him with your goals and timelines. Remember that when God calls you to step into something new, it's not going to be comfortable at first. Give it time!

2. Welcome Jesus into your most vulnerable areas. Sitting at His feet means that you invite Him and incorporate Him into every aspect of your life. Check the order of your priorities, ensuring that He is first.

3. To live on purpose, develop a daily routine that sets you up for success. Explore the Seven-Day Solitude Plan as an option for helping you to spend time with God and meditate on His Word every day. You can find the Seven-Day Solitude Plan in the Appendix.

Contrary to what we tend to believe, spending time with God will not just happen. It's a discipline that we need to pursue intentionally. When we are intentional about spending time in the bible on a daily basis, a habit will form. Once a habit forms, the spiritual practice of spending time in God's Word will become a normal part of our lifestyle.

Chapter Three Notes

Take some time to unpack all
your takeaways from this chapter

_____

_____

_____

_____

_____

_____

_____

_____

_____

_____

_____

_____

_____

_____

_____

Understand That You Are Chosen

She was brave enough to believe she was loved by
God. And so, she lived every day courageously.
—Estreanda Yates

As Christians, we often say to one another, "You are
chosen!" or "I am chosen!" but I wonder if we truly know
what these words mean for ourselves. For years, I was
simply repeating what other Christians and teachers
around me were saying without truly reflecting on what it
meant to be chosen. We need to understand this truth for
ourselves and not just as something we once heard in a
sermon. I used to wrestle with those words, "You are
chosen." It wasn't until I started to study the Word of God
that I understood their meaning and they became
transformational in how I live my life.

The *U* in our P.U.R.P.O.S.E. acronym stands for
"Understand that you are chosen," so let's begin unfolding
that truth.

Question: Before we get started, take a moment to reflect. What do the words "you are chosen" mean to you right now?

_____

_____

_____

_____

_____

_____

This chapter is about your identity. Before we dig into what Scripture has to say about who you are, I want you to have an idea of what you currently believe about yourself. When we recognize the areas of our lives where we are believing lies, we can then replace those lies with the truth of who God says we are.

Limited by the Lies We Believe

Some of the lies we believe about ourselves come from things other people have said about us. I once took a class that was about learning your leadership style. The objective was to help us, the students, to use our talents. We were encouraged to take a leap of faith to try things we thought we were talented in. The instructor, a respected Bible teacher and pastor, told me that I wasn't a leader and that I needed to stick to administrative roles— in front of my entire class! It was mortifying, and it left me confused and questioning whether God had given me the ability to lead.

When I was a junior in high school, I had a teacher who told me that I would never be a writer. She unapologetically gave me an *F* in her class. I didn't realize how much that experience affected me until many years later, when I heard myself saying things like, "I'm not a writer" and "I don't write well."

Then the Lord put it on my heart to write this book. He chose me, someone who "isn't a writer," to write! Today, by the grace of God, I am a writer and a teacher. And wouldn't you know, I'm a leader as well!

People told me that I wasn't a leader or a writer, and I validated those words in the way I lived my life. Jesus, however, was telling me the exact opposite in what He was calling me to step out and do. We need to understand that the limiting beliefs other people place on us are not God's truth.

We don't have to be confined by these limitations. We can choose not to let them control us. We can choose to live outside the box in which other people try to place us and embrace the opportunities we believe were made for us.

Remember that you are chosen! God is calling you to a distinct purpose. That is the truth, and it will never be a lie. Even when you don't feel like it's true, you can act in faith.

For example, there are plenty of days when I don't feel able or equipped, days when I have woken up with feelings of doubt and discouragement. However, I choose not to let my feelings rule my life. Instead, I live out God's truth over my life by faith. I look at what's in my control, and I choose to act on what I believe is the right thing to do, regardless of how I'm feeling.

Imagine having an infant and waking up one day not in the mood to take care of your baby. If you were to allow those feelings to dictate your actions, the consequences would be unfathomable! Infants cannot meet their basic needs on their own. They need a parent or guardian's help to meet their physical and emotional needs every day. They need love and devotion to survive and thrive.

Let's be real. If you're a parent, you know that there are moments when you don't feel like fulfilling your parenting responsibilities. What do you do? You place your feelings to the side and do what you know is the right thing to do. You pick up your child and meet his or her needs. In those moments, you experience a depth of sacrificial love that you didn't know you had in you. When your child smiles at you, you remember your "why," and your desire to love your child with all of your heart returns tenfold.

It's a similar process of decision-making when you choose to devote your life to a particular calling. You have to find a way to nurture your passion in all seasons. You have to give it your time and attention as if it will die if you don't. You have to choose not to abandon it when things get hard. You have to choose to give it your all even when it doesn't seem like it's giving you anything back in return. You have to choose to give it your time and your best effort in spite of opposition.

Jesus didn't necessarily feel like going to the cross. He actually asked the Father if there was any other way

(Matthew 26:39; Mark 14:35–36; Luke 22:41–42). But in obedience to the Father, Jesus did the right thing, and His decision was one of the most impactful decisions ever made. Millions upon millions of lives have been forever changed and will continue to change because of His obedience. Our choices impact our lives and the people around us. Choose to do what you know you should do.

I would like to lead you through an exercise to help you identify the lies you have believed about yourself and replace them with truth. This activity has the power to uncover some deep wounds, but it also has the power to bind up those wounds with the words of truth necessary for healing.

Activity: Replacing Lies with Truth

Grab your laptop, your journal, or a piece of paper and work through the steps below.

1) Set a timer for ten minutes. Take that time to reflect on the following questions and write down your responses.

   a. What are some of the things people have said about you that have hurt you?

   b. What are some negative things you have said about yourself, your body, and your life?

   c. What negative things have you believed about God's plan for your life?

    d. What doubts about who you are resurface continually in your mind?

2) Set the timer for another ten minutes. Now, using a different color of pen or font, replace the lies with truth. As you read through every lie you wrote down, pretend that Jesus is beside you, whispering the truth to you. Cross out each lie or constraining belief and, next to it, write what Jesus would say instead.

    a. Here's an example of what the truth might look like: *"Daughter, I have given you everything you need to do and what I have called you to do. You are chosen. You are loved. Don't worry. I am with you."*

As you complete this exercise, notice that sometimes when we're doubting ourselves, we're really doubting God. We're questioning who He is and what He is able and willing to do in us and in our lives. That was a hard lesson for me to learn. Before I began pursuing my passion, I wondered if it could truly become a reality. What I was really asking myself was whether I could make it happen. The truth is that I can't make anything happen, but God can. I can't control the outcome, but God can. It was a powerful moment when I realized that my self-doubt was really my doubt in God and His ability to be strength in my weakness. I was doubting His ability to give me a vision and carry me through to the end.

I also had to acknowledge that what I want to happen might not happen. Learning to go through the process without knowing if the outcome would meet my expectations was a hard reality for me. I had to learn to commit to the process and surrender the results to God.

> **True courage is taking a leap of faith without really knowing the outcome.**

I hope that Jesus used the activity above to speak transformative truth into your life. This battle against lies is ongoing. There will always be an enemy looking to attack you in unprotected places. We need to protect the vulnerable areas of our hearts and lives.

Instead of suppressing our vulnerabilities, we need to recognize them and proclaim truth over them. We need to pursue healing so we can be victorious. We also need to surround ourselves with other believers who are stronger in our areas of weakness, people who can teach us and encourage us. Once we are armed with the truth, we can leave our fear behind and step onto the battlefield in faith.

A Letter from God

Let's dig deeper into what Scripture says about our identity. We will be reading Ephesians 1:1–8 to discover what it means to be chosen by God. This is a rich and beautifully written passage, and I really want it to resonate with you. To that end, I have replaced the words *us* and *our* with *you* and *your*.

I want you to read this Scripture passage like it's a letter written to you, because in many ways, it is. I want you to read this passage as if your heavenly Father, your greatest advocate, your best friend, the Creator of the universe, is telling you who you are and what you have—because He is!

This letter is from Paul, chosen by the will of God to be an apostle of Christ Jesus.

I am writing to God's holy people in Ephesus, who are faithful followers of Christ Jesus.

May God [your] Father and the Lord Jesus Christ give you grace and peace.

All praise to God, the Father of [your] Lord Jesus Christ, who has blessed [you] with every spiritual blessing in the heavenly realms because [you] are united with Christ. Even before he made the world, God loved [you] and chose [you] in Christ to be holy and without fault in his eyes. God decided in advance to adopt [you] into his own family by bringing [you] to himself through Jesus Christ. This is what he wanted to do, and it gave him great pleasure. So ... praise God for the glorious grace he has poured out on [you] who belong to his dear Son. He is so rich in kindness and grace that he purchased [your] freedom with the blood of his Son and forgave [your] sins. He has showered his kindness on [you], along with all wisdom and understanding.

—Ephesians 1:1–8 (NLT)

Paul, inspired by the Holy Spirit, wrote this letter to the believers at the church of Ephesus. Look at how Paul addressed the Ephesians in verse 1. He referred to them as "God's holy people." The New King James Version reads "saints" (Ephesians 1:1 NKJV). The same is true of you. If you are in Christ, you are one of God's holy people. You are a saint.

We see our flaws and our failures, but
God sees us as the pinnacle of His creation.

That's kind of a big deal! Saints are holy. We are God's most precious possession (1 Peter 2:9). Isn't that amazing? Even though we fall short of perfection all the time, God sees us as His most prized possession.

We Are Defined by Grace

In verse 2, Paul prayed that the Ephesian believers would have both grace and peace. These qualities are essential to the Christian life. Some of us have convinced ourselves that we should be walking in guilt and shame. Many Christians do not understand who they are in Christ, and they doubt their value. They don't believe that they are truly forgiven.

God gives us His grace, His undeserved favor, as a free gift so that we don't have to walk in guilt and shame. Instead, we can walk in grace. Grace is a free gift for us because God already paid for it with the blood of His Son. When Jesus died for us, the blood He shed on the cross paid for our sins and shortcomings. They do not have to be paid for again.

You don't have to believe the lie that you aren't good enough to be called by God and to have a personal relationship with Him. God's grace comes with His complete forgiveness, His unfailing love, and His promises over our lives. His grace covers our shame and guilt and gives us the confidence to move forward, knowing that He has a purpose for us. God's love and grace never come to an end; they never run out.

The proof that God has paid for this grace is right there in the promises He gave us in Scripture. The fruit that He produces in our lives and the testimonies of believers bear witness to the truth of His Word and His unfailing love. You are not defined by your past, your failures, what others say about you, or the lies you believe about yourself. You are defined by God's grace.

God's Grace Protects Us

Not only does God's grace define us, but it protects us as well. Even if a situation ends in heartache or disappointment, His grace still protects us. Sometimes we don't get what we want when we want it. We have to keep trusting that God really does have good in store for us. His grace is there for us in every disappointment.

Sometimes we don't get what we want because God has something better for us. I once applied for the same administrative position three times, and all three times, I was turned down for the job. It was heartbreaking and discouraging, especially since I couldn't understand why God wasn't giving me the job.

The first two times I interviewed for the position, I

received a phone call from Human Resources thanking me for interviewing and letting me know that they had decided to move forward with other candidates. Each time, I politely thanked them for the phone call and the opportunity to interview, but I felt far from thankful. I felt rejected. I believed that I was perfect for the position. I had all of the qualifications they were looking for and then some! I couldn't understand why they wouldn't hire me.

The third time I applied, I didn't even get an interview. I had spoken with the person who was leaving the position, and she assured me that she had already convinced her boss that I was the perfect candidate. So I applied for the job yet again, with full anticipation that I would be hearing from Human Resources to schedule an interview.

I never got that call, and a few weeks later, the position was filled by someone I knew very well. We both served at our church on a regular basis. I wanted to be happy for her, but I wasn't. I tried to convince myself that she was the perfect fit for the position, but deep down, I believed that she was in the position I was supposed to have. I was extremely disappointed that even though I was seemingly the perfect candidate, I didn't even get an interview.

A few years later, the company I worked for gave me a promotion and a raise, along with the first right of refusal to own the company if the owner decided to sell it. Not only that, but when I had my baby, the CEO built me an office so that I could bring my baby in with me whenever I needed to. I now realize that God closed doors that I really wanted to open because He was going to open doors that I never knew existed.

What we see as rejection and disappointment might really be God's grace, protection, and guidance. We don't always see His grace right away, but we need to trust that His will is for our good. That's where faith comes into the picture.

I had to reject the idea that I was a reject. Time allowed space for healing, but it also revealed that God had something better for me. Time is a precious gift. Some healing takes time, and we cannot rush it.

> ### *It's important to separate our circumstances from our identity.*

Today I am thankful that God closed those doors because missing out on those opportunities brought me to where I am today and created a path for me that has brought me great joy. I know beyond a shadow of a doubt that the administrative position I was seeking was not the opportunity God had for me. I can now confidently say that the lady who has that position is supposed to be there, and I *am* happy for her!

God's Grace Gives Us His Best

What's your story? Perhaps there are some doors that God has not opened for you, and you need to trust that He will open the right doors at the right time. Perhaps you need to start knocking on doors and stop fearing rejection, or maybe you need to recover from a door that God has closed. Ask Him to help you heal and give you wisdom to move forward.

Grace means that God has given us the power to live the life He has for us, to live with P.U.R.P.O.S.E., and to do what He has called us to do. It doesn't mean that we will always get our way or that things will always turn out the way we want them to.

We don't need to be jealous of what others have, because we, too, have someone looking out for our best interests. We can move ahead with confidence, knowing that God's grace will open the right doors as we continue to follow His guidance in faithful obedience. His grace will also protect us by closing any doors that we are not meant to enter. If we trust in God's love, wisdom, and grace and choose to move forward in faith, even when we cannot see how everything will come together, God will provide for us and protect us in amazing ways.

We need to continue proclaiming God's truth over our lives. We are chosen, and no circumstance we walk through can ever change the irrevocable truth of who we are in Christ.

The Truth About You

Now that we have explored the concept of grace mentioned in Ephesians 1:2, let's continue digging into the rest of the verses in this passage to find out more about our identity in Christ. Ephesians 1:4 gives us one of the most important takeaways: "... He chose us in Him before the foundation of the world, that we should be holy and without blame before Him in love" (NKJV).

> *Truth does not change; it remains*
> *the same even if we change our minds.*

I want you to sit with this truth for a moment: you are chosen. Before there even was a world, God chose you in Christ to be His own. That is a fact. That is truth.

In today's society, some people believe that they can and should redefine reality based on their personal feelings, but that's not the way truth works. Ten people can look at the same picture of a chair and see it differently, but none of them can honestly deny that it's a picture of a chair. If I wake up one day and decide that the picture of a chair is really a picture of a table, that doesn't change the nature of the picture. It's still a picture of a chair, regardless of what I want it to be or what I want to call it.

Likewise, you are chosen by God, no matter how you happen to feel about yourself on any given day. He chose you, and then He created you. It would be foolish to think that God chose you and created you with such love and intricacy but didn't bother to give you a purpose. You had a purpose before you were even created.

God chose you because He loves you. He wants your life to reflect His glory and holiness as you live in the freedom of His forgiveness and grace. You are chosen and wanted!

> *Walking in your identity is not a destination,*
> *but rather a lifelong pursuit.*

The more you act in faith, the more your belief in who you are in Jesus and how much He loves you will grow. Take a moment to say to yourself, *"I am chosen."*

Question: In your own words—not words that you have heard in church or from other Christians, but the words that Jesus has truly and undeniably spoken to your own heart—write a description of who God says you are. If the answer is not clear to you, ask Jesus to speak over you and reveal to you, without a doubt, your identity in Him.

_____

_____

_____

_____

_____

_____

You Have Been Adopted into God's Family

We are not only chosen, but also adopted. Ephesians 1:5 tells us that God "predestined us to adoption as sons by Jesus Christ to Himself, according to the good pleasure of His will" (NKJV). God knew you in your mother's womb, and He chose to adopt you into His family. He knew the decisions and mistakes you would make, yet He still chose you.

The word *adoption* can carry different connotations for different people, depending on their experiences with adoption. For some, it's a word that fills them with gratitude. For others, it's a painful word that rips the bandage off of an open wound.

The truth is that God invented the idea of adoption so that we could experience Him as our Father. The most beautiful adoption stories in this world are those that reflect the heart of God. People adopt children so that they can give them a life they would otherwise never have and a family they can call their own.

Just as parents have to pay various fees associated with adoption before they can bring their child home, Jesus paid for our sins with His blood so that He could make us part of His family. God's adoption of believers is evidence that He accepts us and has handpicked us for a purpose. We belong. *You* belong.

When we understand that God has adopted us as His beloved children, we can cope with whatever lies ahead because we know that we are not alone. We can live as people who are wanted, as people who belong to God, because that is the truth of who we are.

Question: How different would your life be if you were to walk as someone who belongs to God? How would this perspective change the way you approach opportunities and relationships? How would it impact your family, business, or ministry?

_____

_____

_____

_____

_____

_____

You Are Equipped to Live a Fruitful Life

I have a confession to make. Before I was married, I adopted two dogs. I still have them, and I still love them, but when my husband and I had our first child, our entire life became about our son. We were consumed with caring for our child, and our dogs were no longer our primary focus.

Thankfully, God doesn't do that with us! There has never been a time in our adoption story when God made us less important because something else became more of a priority. He chose us, He adopted us into His family, and then He equipped us with the tools we would need to live fruitful lives.

Ephesians 1:3 says, "Blessed be the God and Father of our Lord Jesus Christ, who has blessed us with every spiritual blessing in the heavenly places in Christ" (NKJV). That's what love does. Love sets us up for success, not failure. You already have everything you need to excel in God's kingdom because God has given you every spiritual blessing.

Ephesians 1:1–9 outlines the spiritual blessings we have as people who are chosen by God. Let's examine these verses more closely.

You are "holy and without blame" (Ephesians 1:4 NKJV). God made you pure so that you could have access to Him. The blessing of being "holy and without blame" means that you never have to worry about God's love for you and His promises to you, because they are not based on what you do or don't do. You can be close to God because you are free and forgiven!

You are "in [God's] love" (Ephesians 1:4 NKJV). You are covered by God's unconditional love. He will always guide you and protect you. God's love has no bounds, and He will never stop loving you. You can come to Him with anything and everything.

You are "accepted in the Beloved" by God's grace (Ephesians 1:6 NKJV). You are accepted, not rejected. You are not an outcast; you belong. God doesn't want you to try to make yourself perfect before you go to Him. Instead, when you believe in His Son, He takes you as you are. Then, in His grace, He challenges and equips you to become more like Jesus every day.

You "have redemption through His blood" (Ephesians 1:7 NKJV). Jesus already paid for your freedom. You could never earn it, and you don't need to do everything you can to be good in the hope of buying it again. Jesus paid the price in full with the perfect sacrifice of His blood, the only acceptable payment. Nothing can top the price He paid for you. The blessing of redemption reveals the truth about your value. Jesus considers you worth dying for!

You have "the forgiveness of sins" (Ephesians 1:7 NKJV). God knew your sins before you did. His forgiveness comes with His unconditional love. You don't have to walk around feeling guilty or ashamed. When you confess your sins to God with a repentant heart, He forgives you completely. Let your sins go! You don't have to carry them around anymore.

You are a child of God. The fact that He chose you to be His child means that He loves you, wants you, values you, accepts you, cherishes you, and forgives you. Can you imagine how different your life would look if you were to embrace the truth of who you are? These are truths we need to keep at the forefront of our minds. We need to look ourselves in the mirror and remind ourselves of these truths regularly.

Our beliefs guide our decisions, and our decisions determine the outcome of our lives. When we know who we are, it will shape our decisions and ultimately our destiny. It is imperative that we not only do the work of learning about our identity in Christ, but also believe the truth of who we are as adopted children of God. There are days, sometimes several times in one day, when I say out loud, "I *am* a child of God!"

Activity: Who Do You Say You Are Now?

Earlier in the chapter, I asked you to write down the lies and negative things you have believed about yourself. Now that we have dug into Scripture in order to understand our identity in Christ, how would you answer the question: What does it mean that you are chosen?

Question: Without rereading Ephesians 1:1–9, answer the question: What does it mean that you are chosen by God?

_____

_____

_____

_____

_____

_____

Take some time to reflect on what you have learned about your God-given identity and fill out the certificate below. I have included an example for you.

Estreanda

She is one whom God has chosen. She is picked and purposed. She has never walked a day in her life unwanted. God is always pursuing her. She is created to move mountains.

An irrevocable truth

In your own words, based on the truth of God's Word, who are you in Christ Jesus?

I am:

-
-
-
-
-
-

Remember that how you feel on any given day doesn't change the truth of who you are. The things that you wrote about yourself in the certificate above are always true. Who you are is based on the truth of who God says you are. It will never change. You are chosen by God! *That is an irrevocable truth!*

Question: Which of the spiritual blessings discussed above stands out to you most? Why?

_____

_____

_____

_____

_____

_____

Question: How can you apply some of the truths you have learned in this chapter to your life?

_____

_____

_____

_____

_____

_____

Get Set! Go!

In this chapter, we pressed into the practical aspects of understanding that you are chosen by God for a life of P.U.R.P.O.S.E.:

1. Identify the lies you have believed about yourself. Then replace them with powerful truths from Scripture.

2. In your own words, define what it means to be

chosen. Often we recite what we have heard in church because it sounds good, but we don't take the time to ask ourselves, *"What does it really mean?"* Being chosen isn't something to recite; it's who you are, and it's important that you truly understand what it means. No one and nothing but God determines your identity. You are chosen, called, and adopted. No matter what you face, you can walk as a woman who has been handpicked by God. That's who you are, and it will never change.

Your identity in Christ doesn't change with the different seasons of life. It's a constant truth that can give you perspective and courage no matter what your temporary circumstances are. At the same time, your identity is a journey you take with Jesus, not a destination you will reach at some point in the future. When you believe in the truth of your identity in Christ and you act in faith, making decisions based on who God says you are, you will see His transformational power in your life.

Chapter Four Notes

*Take some time to unpack all
your takeaways from this chapter*

_____

_____

_____

_____

_____

_____

_____

_____

_____

_____

_____

_____

_____

_____

_____

_____

CHAPTER FIVE

Rest in the Storm

You have turned my mourning into joyful
dancing. You have taken away my clothes of
mourning and clothed me with joy…
—Psalm 30:11 (NLT)

Storms are unexpected difficulties in our lives over
which we have no control. They are an inevitable part of
life, and we cannot dictate when they will come, how long
they will last, or how strong they will be. The only thing
we can control is how we respond to these storms.

Storms have the potential to derail us as we pursue our
God-given dreams. Our discouragement mounts as the
difficulties and disappointments pile up, and we focus on
trying to control the uncontrollable instead of doing what
we can and trusting God to do what we cannot.

The *R* in our P.U.R.P.O.S.E. acronym stands for "Rest
in the storm." Mark 4:35–41 (NKJV) shows us how Jesus'

disciples responded when they found themselves in the midst of an unexpected storm—literally:

> *On the same day, when evening had come, He said to them, "Let us cross over to the other side." Now when they had left the multitude, they took Him along in the boat as He was. And other little boats were also with Him. And a great windstorm arose, and the waves beat into the boat, so that it was already filling. But He was in the stern, asleep on a pillow. And they awoke Him and said to Him, "Teacher, do You not care that we are perishing?"*
>
> *Then He arose and rebuked the wind, and said to the sea, "Peace, be still!" And the wind ceased and there was a great calm. But He said to them, "Why are you so fearful? How is it that you have no faith?" And they feared exceedingly, and said to one another, "Who can this be, that even the wind and the sea obey Him!"*

Earlier that day, Jesus taught the multitudes and His disciples, sharing with them the parable of the sower (Mark 4:1–9). Once He was alone with His disciples, He explained the meaning of the parable of the sower and shared the parables of the growing seed and the mustard seed (Mark 4:10–34). Following all of these teachings, Jesus decided that He would take the disciples out on a boat.

I don't think that the teaching stopped on the boat. For the disciples, the teaching became more tangible on the boat. Jesus also used the storm to teach a timeless principle that would guide us all in finding freedom when we are hit with the most difficult times in our lives.

All You Can Do Is Rest

I didn't grow up with my mother and father. Both of my parents were on drugs, and I lived with my grandmother. My mother became sober when I was in elementary school, and by the time I was in sixth grade, my mother had been sober long enough that I was allowed to live with her. I remember being a little girl and going out to bring my mom and dad a meal my grandmother had cooked for them. I don't remember them having a home at that time. I remember bringing them a plate of food out on the street, where I believed they lived.

I was in a situation I didn't ask for and couldn't control. If the choice had been mine, I would have wanted to live with my mom and dad. My situation could have resulted in bitterness and resentment. I could have been angry with God and my parents, but I wasn't. I never felt that I had a bad life. I am exceedingly thankful for the love my grandmother gave to me by providing me with a safe home. I'm thankful that my parents, even in their drug addiction, loved me and wanted the best for me. My parents were granted visiting rights, and I absolutely loved the weekends I got to be with them.

Sometimes we find ourselves in situations that we didn't choose for ourselves. However, every circumstance in our lives, even the ones we don't choose but God allows, has the power to teach us something valuable that we can learn only from that particular experience. My childhood taught me how to have a little grit in life, and I learned that I can find meaning and purpose in everything that comes my way. I also learned that it's always possible to move forward in life, regardless of the obstacles.

When the disciples found themselves out on a boat in the middle of a terrifying storm, it wasn't by accident. Jesus had something to teach them. Mark 4:38 always makes me laugh: "But He was in the stern, asleep on a pillow" (NKJV). The storm was getting worse, the disciples were panicking, and Jesus was taking a nap. He even had a pillow! He wasn't just resting in the storm; He was resting comfortably.

Jesus perfectly embodied "the peace of God, which surpasses all understanding" described in Philippians 4:7 (NKJV). This peace comes from God alone. He grants it to us when we seek His perspective and present our requests to Him through prayer (Philippians 4:6).

Perspective is powerful.
When God gives us His perspective,
His perspective gives us hope!

The lesson here is simple but supernatural. Once you recognize that you are in a storm—in a difficult situation that is beyond your control—and you have done everything you can do, it's time to rest. That doesn't mean sitting on the edge of your seat, biting your nails, wondering how you're going to make it through this situation. Instead of worrying, rest comfortably in the supernatural peace of God that surpasses all understanding.

For me, resting looks different in different situations.

Sometimes it's acceptance, and sometimes it's surrender. Sometimes it's choosing to trust God. Other times, it's allowing time and patience to heal my wounds.

Resting in the Lord doesn't mean ignoring your situation or how you feel. You need to acknowledge your emotions, name them, and allow yourself to feel them. Pray and connect with the Lord as you feel every ounce of your pain.

Rest by asking God for help and healing. Seek help from Him and from the people He has put in your life to love and support you. Rest in the Lord by choosing to believe that His promises for your life are still true, even when you cannot yet see the purpose of what you are experiencing. Acknowledge your past and your present and seek God's will for how best to move forward.

When we think of rest, we may see it as passive, but resting in the Lord requires an intentional decision. It means choosing to trust that He sees the bigger picture and is working all of it out for your good (Romans 8:28). Resting is not sitting and twiddling your thumbs; it's connecting with God in all of your trials. It's relying on the truth of God's Word and believing in who He says He is and who He says you are.

Resting in the midst of a storm is not the lazy choice or the easy way out. Resting in the Lord goes against our natural inclinations. It's much easier for us to worry. Instead, God wants us to follow Jesus' example and do the harder thing by resting. When we choose rest over worry and peace over panic, we are demonstrating our faith that God is with us and will guide us, teach us, and strengthen us through every circumstance. We can move forward with hope, doing what we can do and trusting God to do the things that only He can do.

> *If you choose to rest in the Lord and*
> *hold on to hope in the thick of the storm,*
> *you can find meaning and purpose,*
> *even in traumatic circumstances.*

Doesn't God Care?

In Mark 4:38, the disciples asked Jesus a question that people often ask in the midst of a storm: "Teacher, do You not care that we are perishing?" (NKJV). Instead of following Jesus' example and resting in the storm, they questioned His care for them. He was the one in charge, so why wasn't He doing anything about the situation?

Jesus responded to His disciples' terror by rebuking the wind and telling the sea to be still (Mark 4:39), and the wind and the sea listened to Him! The wind stopped howling, and the water became calm.

The disciples were still trying to figure out who Jesus was. Their apparent shock in Mark 4:41—"Who can this be, that even the wind and the sea obey Him!" (NKJV)—shows that they had a very limited view of Jesus. Wasn't He their Savior in their moment of need? In the disciples' moment of crisis, they, like many of us, saw that things were getting worse instead of better and doubted that Jesus still had their best interest at heart.

Up to this point, Jesus' disciples might have thought of Him as a really good teacher or a healer. They might not

ON PURPOSE · 103

have thought of Him as the God who controls the earth and rules over the wind and the waves. Though Jesus' disciples had seen Him heal the sick and cast out demons, they had not seen Him control creation. Through this experience, they realized that Jesus was so much more than who they thought He was.

God is the One who allows the storms to come, and He is the One who has the ability to quiet the storms. We can find peace in the midst of storms when we trust that He is sovereign over them.

Right before I had my son Braven, I had a miscarriage. It's hard to capture in words what I felt, the grief that gripped me. There is nothing like it. I remember going into the hospital and seeing a little baby that was forming but didn't have a heartbeat. The doctor told us that they couldn't detect a heartbeat and requested that we come back the following day to get a second opinion.

My husband and I clung to each other and prayed for a miracle. We prayed that when we went back into the hospital to get the second opinion, there would be a heartbeat. I wanted to see a heartbeat more than anything else I had ever wanted. I had already started planning how we would decorate our baby's room. I didn't want to face the reality that I wasn't going to be able to carry this child to full term.

The next day, we got a second opinion, and it was confirmed that our little sprout didn't make it. I was faced with the unbearable task of choosing how to let my baby go. The doctors gave me two choices regarding how to let the baby pass. I didn't want to choose either option. I wanted my baby to stay safely tucked in my womb. I wanted my baby to keep growing. I wanted my baby to live.

I didn't think that I would ever have to make this type of decision. I didn't think that things could get worse. I was in the boat, and like the disciples, I felt a flood come into a space that should have been safe. I was about to drown in heartache. I couldn't figure out why God would let this happen.

Why would He allow me to dream and then take it away? *I still don't know why.* Sometimes when terrible things happen, we don't know why. We may come to understand in time, or we may never have the answer. But in that moment, I remember praying. I prayed for a peace that would surpass my understanding, and even though I still didn't understand, God gave me peace and hope.

I reached out to people who had suffered the same traumatic experience, and I walked through my emotions every single day. Some days I felt like I was okay, and other days I was drowning in anger, frustration, questions, and confusion.

I know that the loss of my child wasn't my fault, and I will never know why God allowed it to happen, but going through that experience taught me to acknowledge and deal directly with painful emotions instead of suppressing them. Before that, I tended to push aside my emotions and move on to the next thing. The loss I suffered taught me the priceless lesson of walking through my pain and pursuing healing. Learning this was the catalyst for me to start facing my fears. I didn't know that this storm would teach me to walk through pain and lead me into the journey of pursuing my God-given passion to teach and encourage other Jesus followers to live on purpose.

Question: Are you currently experiencing a hardship? What is one truth you learned from how Jesus and His disciples responded to the storm when they were on the boat?

_____

_____

_____

_____

_____

_____

Question: Consider a storm you have faced in the past. How did you get through it? How did you change as a result of the experience? Did God use that situation to teach you something that you wouldn't otherwise have learned?

_____

_____

_____

_____

_____

_____

Question: What are some ways you can use what you learned in the storm to help other people?

_____

_____

_____

_____

_____

_____

Question: Have you, perhaps unintentionally, put limits on God in your own life? Are you allowing doubt, fear, and anger to hold you back? In what areas of your life are you doubting God's power and authority?

_____

_____

_____

_____

_____

Question: Why are you so fearful in these areas of your life? I want you to go deeper with this and ask God to show you the root. What is keeping you from living by faith?

_____

_____

_____

_____

_____

_____

Let Go of Fear and Focus on God

When Jesus asked a question in Scripture, it wasn't because He didn't know the answer. It was to get to the root of an issue and make people think. I encourage you to ask yourself the same questions that Jesus asked His disciples in Mark 4:40: "Why are you so fearful? How is it that you have no faith?" (NKJV). I have asked myself these questions several times in my life, and whenever I answer them truthfully, they bring revelation.

> **Resting in the storm means having faith that God will take care of us.**

I remember the day I watched my uncle trying to teach my niece how to swim. She was terrified of the water because of a previous bad experience. She just wanted him to let her go so that she could return to the shallow end, which she saw as the safe part of the water. She wanted her feet to touch the ground. She wanted to feel in control of her safety.

However, my uncle knew that my niece wouldn't learn to swim unless she could overcome her fear of the deep end. He went to the shallow part of the pool, gently picked her up, and carried her to deeper waters. She was now beyond the point where her feet could touch the bottom of the pool. She wasn't in control. My uncle, wanting desperately to help her overcome her fear, held her close and did everything he could to assure her that she was okay. Even though she was safe in his strong arms, she was shaking with fear.

Finally, my uncle loosened his grip on her just enough that she could look him in the eye, and he spoke to her in a stern tone because he wanted her to hear him and believe him. He said, "I love you, and I am not going to let you drown." You could see the impact of his words and the surrender in her heart as her face instantly became more relaxed.

In this moment, I could tell that my niece made a decision to trust my uncle. He managed to get her attention and speak past her fears. His assurance gave my niece the faith to take a deep breath and relax her tense muscles. A few minutes later, she was splashing around in the water as my uncle held her in his arms, and she was having the time of her life!

Some truly terrible and hurtful things have happened to us and to people in our lives. It would be insensitive and incorrect to say that God allowed those storms to happen in order to teach someone a specific lesson.

Learning to rest in the storm is about finding the space where you can trust in God's sovereignty, no matter the circumstance, because this is the place where you will experience freedom, healing, and divine perspective.

God wants us to be free from our fears. He wants us to live with hope and power. We can feel fear and decide not to be controlled by it. We don't have to allow fear to keep us from exploring uncharted territory and all that God has for us. He wants to reassure us that we don't have to be afraid. If we would just let His Word pierce through our fears and trust that He won't let us drown when we feel like we're sinking, we would find meaning in the hardest of times and faith in the most fearful situations.

Activity: Where You End and God Begins

Storms are unexpected difficulties that are outside of our control. They go beyond our human intellect and any earthly wisdom we can acquire. It's important for us to recognize whether we are in a storm or we are experiencing the consequences of our own poor decisions. Once we have determined that we are in a storm, we need to distinguish between what we can do to help manage the storm and what is in God's hands.

Take some time to fill out the chart below. Keeping in mind the dreams that God has placed in your heart, identify what you are afraid of and why, what is in God's control, and what is in your control. I have included an example to help you get started.

Things in my life that are causing me to have worry and fear:	The items that are in God's control:	What's in my control:
Are we doing the right things with our children? Will the women's conference be a failure? If I step out in faith, will my family be okay?		

Filling in this chart should help you to get a better idea of where your human abilities end and God's power begins and encourage you to rest in the midst of the storm.

Discovering what it means to rest in Him in the midst of life's storms will make all the difference.

I also encourage you to memorize one or more of the following scriptures about peace:

- "Let the peace of Christ rule in your hearts, since as members of one body you were called to peace. And be thankful" (Colossians 3:15 NIV).

- "Do not be anxious about anything, but in every situation, by prayer and petition, with thanksgiving, present your requests to God. And the peace of God, which transcends all understanding, will guard your hearts and your minds in Christ Jesus" (Philippians 4:6–7 NIV).

- "The LORD gives strength to his people; the LORD blesses his people with peace" (Psalm 29:11 NIV).

When you're feeling overwhelmed by a storm, these scriptures will help you to remember that Christ is the source of your peace. As you pursue the dreams that God has laid on your heart and continue to live with P.U.R.P.O.S.E., you will encounter storms of many kinds. If you choose to trust God's sovereignty, you will find supernatural peace in life's most difficult and chaotic moments.

> **Question:** In your own words, what does resting in the storm mean to you? Can you apply this concept to a situation you are currently experiencing?

Get Set! Go!

In this chapter, we learned how to respond with P.U.R.P.O.S.E to unexpected difficulties in our lives over which we have no control:

1. Once you recognize that you are in a storm and you have done everything you can do, rest comfortably in the supernatural peace of God that surpasses all understanding. Rest by walking through your pain and facing your emotions. Rest

by relying on God for help and healing. Rest with the truth about what happened to you and ask God how to move forward.

2. When something happens and you don't know why, accept that you may never know why. In such moments, reach out to your inner circle or the people he has placed in your life and let them know you're having a difficult time. Engage with the Lord and pray for peace, healing, and divine perspective and let God's word fill you with hope.

3. Cling to God as you press through your pain and fears to live life with passion and purpose.

Chapter Five Notes

*Take some time to unpack all
your takeaways from this chapter*

_____

_____

_____

_____

_____

_____

_____

_____

_____

_____

_____

_____

_____

_____

_____

_____

_____

_____

CHAPTER SIX

Pick Up Your Bed and Walk

Leaving behind nights of terror and fear / I rise /
Into a daybreak that's wondrously clear / I rise…
I rise.[6]

—Maya Angelou

Sometimes we get to a point in our lives where we feel
stuck. We don't know how to move forward in pursuit of
the dreams that God has placed in our hearts. We end up
sitting around, waiting for things to happen on their own,
instead of taking action.

The second *P* in our P.U.R.P.O.S.E. acronym stands
for "Pick up your bed and walk." The key to this part of
the acronym is found in John 5:1–15, which tells of how
Jesus healed a man who had been sick for thirty-eight
years. You will be blown away by the powerful and
practical principles in these scriptures. This Scripture
passage has drastically changed my life, and I believe that
it can do the same for you. Let's read it!

After this there was a feast of the Jews, and Jesus went up to Jerusalem. Now there is in Jerusalem by the Sheep Gate a pool, which is called in Hebrew, Bethesda, having five porches. In these lay a great multitude of sick people, blind, lame, paralyzed, waiting for the moving of the water. For an angel went down at a certain time into the pool and stirred up the water; then whoever stepped in first, after the stirring of the water, was made well of whatever disease he had. Now a certain man was there who had an infirmity thirty-eight years. When Jesus saw him lying there, and knew that he already had been in that condition a long time, He said to him, "Do you want to be made well?"

The sick man answered Him, "Sir, I have no man to put me into the pool when the water is stirred up; but while I am coming, another steps down before me."

Jesus said to him, "Rise, take up your bed and walk." And immediately the man was made well, took up his bed, and walked.

And that day was the Sabbath. The Jews therefore said to him who was cured, "It is the Sabbath; it is not lawful for you to carry your bed."

He answered them, "He who made me well said to me, 'Take up your bed and walk.'"

Then they asked him, "Who is the Man who said to you, 'Take up your bed and walk'?" But the one who was healed did not know who it was, for Jesus

*had withdrawn, a multitude being in that place.
Afterward Jesus found him in the temple, and said
to him, "See, you have been made well. Sin no
more, lest a worse thing come upon you."*

*The man departed and told the Jews that it was
Jesus who had made him well.*

—*John 5:1–15 (NKJV)*

**It's time to stop waiting and start
moving in the direction you believe
in your heart you are supposed to go.**

It's time for you to rise from a position of paralysis and
move from waiting to walking!

You Are Surrounded by Mercy and Grace

John 5:2 tells us two very important details about the
environment in which this healing took place. First, the
name of the pool was Bethesda, which means "house of
mercy."[7,8] Second, the pool had five porches, and in the
Bible, five is the number of grace.[9] This man was
surrounded by mercy and grace. He had everything he
needed to take a step of faith, yet he had convinced
himself that he was stuck and could not move.

Scripture is not specific about the nature of the man's
illness. John 5:5 says that he "had an infirmity thirty-eight
years" (NKJV). It was likely a physical illness or condition
that affected his mobility, as it was difficult for him to get

into the pool without help (John 5:7).

Some scholars think that the man's paralysis might have been the result of sin.[10] This is implied in Scripture by what Jesus said to the man after He healed him: "See, you have been made well. Sin no more, lest a worse thing come upon you" (John 5:14 NKJV).

Jesus was an expression of both mercy and grace to this man, despite the sin he had been living in for the past thirty-eight years. Jesus gave him freedom and enabled him to rise and walk, even if he didn't deserve it.

You have the ability to move in the direction Jesus is calling you. His grace and mercy are all you really need.

You may not be lying by the pool of Bethesda in one of the five porches, but you are in the same environment as that man. You are surrounded by mercy and sitting in grace. You don't have to do anything to earn or deserve that mercy and grace. God has given them to you, no strings attached.

God Sees You

John 5:3 describes all of the people waiting for healing by the pool of Bethesda: "In these lay a great multitude of sick people, blind, lame, paralyzed, waiting for the moving of the water" (NKJV). Though this man was surrounded by other people who were also suffering, God saw him.

This is true for you, too. In a world filled with people, God sees you! He sees you, and He does not miss a single moment of your life.

In my walk with Christ, I have found that it's easy to believe this to be true for someone else, but much more challenging to believe it for myself. In order to take hold of the freedom that God has for us and move forward, we need to embrace the truth that God sees each of us. We tend to ignore the bountiful grace and mercy God offers us, because we find it easier to shoulder a burden of doubt, guilt, and shame.

Perhaps that's where your freedom is today. Maybe you need to answer the same question that Jesus asked this man: "Do you want to be made well?" (John 5:6 NKJV). In order to answer this question, you need to acknowledge what is holding you back and be honest with yourself about whether you want God to free you from it. Sometimes we get comfortable with our infirmities and don't truly want to be healed, because that would mean stepping into unfamiliar territory.

I was once in Haiti, leading a mission trip with my husband, and the Lord spoke to my heart. He showed me that fear was holding me back. My life showed a pattern of running from potential rejection or failure. I would only engage in things that I knew I was able to do well. If I was going to live fully in the calling God had for me, I needed freedom from my fear.

When it came to teaching, I hated the thought of missing the mark, and I avoided it at all costs. I wanted to control what other people thought of me, and standing in the shadows, doing and saying all of the right things, was how I accomplished that.

I was afraid that people would see that I wasn't the superhuman spiritual giant they might have thought I was. I was afraid that when people really got to know me, they would realize that I struggled with a lot of the same things they did. I wanted to control what other people thought of me so badly that it kept me paralyzed and stuck, just like that man sitting by the pool of Bethesda.

I remember reading this story and thinking to myself, *"I'm not just reading about this man. I am like this man, sitting and waiting for my opportunity to come, making excuses."* I went to Jesus and said, *"Lord, fear is an issue in my life, and I want to be healed."*

Question: What in your own heart is holding you back and keeping you in bondage? Bring it to Jesus. He is asking you, "Do you want to be healed?" What is your response?

_____

_____

_____

_____

_____

_____

Jesus spoke words of life over this man, and he rose, picked up his bed, and walked. He did this because Jesus told him that he could—and you can, too! God wants you to live the life He has for you. I believe that He is with you and telling you to rise and move forward in the areas of your life where, like this man, you have allowed yourself to believe that you have no power, no help, and no opportunity. I want you to believe that you can rise, pick up your bed, and walk. In every paralyzed area of your life, Jesus is calling you to walk with Him and explore uncharted territory.

Fear Can Keep Us in Bondage

It's interesting to consider that the people at the pool of Bethesda were "blind, lame, [and] paralyzed" (John 5:3 NKJV). Metaphorically speaking, these issues are all side effects of fear. Fear limits our ability to see God (blindness), hinders our ability to move and walk with God (lameness), and keeps us stuck and unable to move (paralysis).

Please don't misunderstand. I am not saying that these people were sick because they were bound by fear. I am saying that their physical issues are a metaphor for what fear can do to us. Fear is bondage, and we need to be released from that bondage.

Question: Take some time to reflect. What areas of your life are controlled by fear? What limiting beliefs or excuses are keeping you trapped in fear?

_____

_____

_____

_____

_____

_____

Question: Be honest with yourself. Do you want to be healed in these areas of your life? Do you want to be able to rise and pursue your God-given passion?

_____

_____

_____

_____

_____

_____

Let me be honest with you. The freedom that comes with healing is not always easy. It doesn't just happen; it's a process in which you have to participate. You have to rise up and commit to living in freedom. The process for me began with studying the Bible to see what it said about fear. Then I started doing things that I knew I should be doing but was avoiding because I was afraid.

This book came from my personal study on fear. The scriptures, insights, and questions are all a part of my personal journey and the process I used to start overcoming my fear of other people's judgment, which kept me from following God's calling for me to teach.

As God revealed His truth to me in the Scriptures, I demonstrated my desire to be truly healed by going to the women's ministry leader at my church and asking if I could teach my series to other women. It was intimidating to take the first step, the second step, and every step after that, but I did it anyway. Moving beyond my fear and following God's calling transformed my life and the lives of the women whom I was privileged to teach each week. The principles in this book were taught in classrooms before they became a book—another intimidating task I said "yes" to. This study was the tool that opened the door for me to teach.

I knew that God didn't want me to hoard the revelations He was giving me; He wanted me to share them. Freedom meant saying "yes" to pursuing the purpose He had placed in my heart, the very thing I had been avoiding out of fear. I had to say 'yes" to studying God's Word and "yes" to seeking and accepting opportunities to serve other women by teaching them what Jesus was teaching me. I had to acknowledge that my fear of failure and not being good enough was holding me back. I had to look my fear in the face and choose not to let it direct my steps when the opportunity to rise was right in front of me.

I am speaking to the dreamer inside of you. Don't let fear win! You have power and authority over your fears, so don't let them control you! There is an infinite army of God's grace and mercy around you and within you. We need to believe that God loves us. He is with us and for us. We need to listen when He speaks to our hearts, saying, *"It's time, and you can."*

What's Your Excuse?

Before we can move forward, we need to get up off our mats. The bed on which the man was lying near the pool of Bethesda was a sleeping mat that he was able to roll or fold up and carry with him when he was healed.

A bed is a place of support and comfort. To some extent, I believe that this man was comfortable in his situation and his excuses. As much as he desired freedom and change, he also had excuses for why he was stuck where he was.

When Jesus asked him if he wanted to be made well, the man didn't answer the question. Instead, he gave Jesus an excuse: "Sir, I have no man to put me into the pool when the water is stirred up; but while I am coming, another steps down before me" (John 5:7 NKJV).

Regardless of how valid his excuse was, it was still an excuse. From this man's perspective, the problems were that no one would help him and other people kept taking his opportunity. He believed that he had the motivation but lacked the means to achieve what he desired. However, the help and opportunities this man thought that he lacked no longer mattered once Jesus came on the scene.

I believe that all of us can relate to this man in some way. We all have been in a place in our lives where we were comfortable in our excuses. At one time or another, we have convinced ourselves that we just needed that certain something to align with our plan in order to achieve the outcome we desired.

I have definitely caught myself thinking like that: *"If I could just get the right mentor, if I could just get that one client, if someone would just believe in me, take me under her wing, and connect me with the resources I need, then things would happen for me."*

The man spent thirty-eight years at the pool of Bethesda, watching other people get what he wanted. Boy, does that sound familiar! So many times, I have scrolled through social media, watching as other people enjoy the opportunities and experiences that I desire. In those moments, I have to ask myself the tough questions. Am I pursuing the things that God has placed in my heart? Am I actively facing my fears and getting out of my comfort zone? Am I doing my part and trusting God with the rest, or am I making excuses? I don't need my perfect plan to fall into place before I move forward. All I need is Jesus' command to "go."

Jesus spoke to this man as if he had everything he needed in order to get the outcome he wanted. Jesus didn't ask the man, "Can you get up?" He commanded the man to get up. This man had the ability to walk; he just needed the faith to stand.

When we get comfortable with being stuck and start making excuses about why we are where we are, our excuses start to become our issues. When we get too comfortable in our issues, our issues start to become our identity, and that's a scary place to be. Trapped by false beliefs, we develop habits that keep our lives stagnant.

You may think that your excuses are valid, and they

very well may be. But as the coach in your corner, I want to challenge you by telling you that any excuse is still an excuse!

> ***Don't let your excuse be the thing***
> ***that keeps you standing still.***

Listen to that still, small voice in your heart, the one that refuses to quit, the one that refuses to let mediocrity take up space in your life. Listen to the voice that whispers, *"God's got you, so go for it!"*

Question: How do you relate to the man lying by the pool of Bethesda? What excuses have you been making? How are you using these excuses to justify why you are staying where you are instead of moving forward on purpose?

_____

_____

_____

_____

_____

_____

From Waiting to Walking

How do we move from sitting in our excuses and waiting for something to happen to walking in freedom? *First, we need to come to terms with the doubts and fears that are preventing us from moving forward and choose to pursue freedom in that area.* Do you fear judgment or rejection? Are you concerned that you won't be able to fulfill what God has called you to do? You need to identify what is holding you back before you can work through it.

Second, we need to recognize our excuses. I often hear Christians say, "I'm just waiting on God." We do need to wait patiently if God's perfect timing has not yet arrived, but we also need to be careful not to put off doing what God is telling us to do just because we don't feel ready to do it. I know that I have used the "waiting on God" excuse when I didn't want to do what God was calling me to do or I was afraid to do it. "I'm waiting on God" or "I'm still praying about it" can sometimes be translated as "I'm waiting on God to change His mind" or "I'm waiting for an option that's more comfortable for me."

We need to be brutally honest with ourselves and make sure that our "waiting" is not linked to a deeply rooted fear or insecurity. If we're using "waiting on God" as an excuse, then we're choosing to stay comfortable when God is telling us to rise.

Third, we need to recognize that moving from waiting to walking requires faith. Instead of acknowledging the man's excuses, Jesus spoke to the man as though he already had the strength to move, as though he already had everything he needed to live the life God was calling him to live.

Jesus didn't ask the man, "Can you get up?" He commanded him to get up. Think about that. When you tell someone to do something, it's because you believe that person has the ability or the potential to do it. I believe with all of my heart that Jesus is speaking to you as well. He is telling you that He has already given you everything you need to acquire the freedom your heart desires.

The issue wasn't the man's circumstances as he thought; it was his faith. People often look at this Scripture passage and focus on the man's lack of faith when he first encountered Jesus, but I believe that it took some serious faith for him to respond to what Jesus said. The man had every reason to doubt that he could get up and walk. He had been paralyzed for thirty-eight years! But in that moment, he set aside his excuses and responded to Jesus' command. He rose, took up his bed, and walked, and his life changed forever.

Fourth, we need to respond to the Word of God and what God is telling us to do. This will require us to:

- Move at the speed of instruction
- "Walk by faith, not by sight" (2 Corinthians 5:7 NKJV)
- Say "yes" to things that sound impossible.

Responding is often the difficult part of this process. We tend to overthink what God is telling us and try to talk ourselves out of it instead of simply following through on what He is asking us to do. We question our capability and the call itself, and we reason ourselves into deciding that we're better off not doing anything at all.

As I have mentioned before, I believe that God is calling me to encourage and equip women to be all that He has created them to be by encouraging them to use their gifts to make things and people in our world better. One of the ways He wants me to do that is by writing this book. I have questioned this calling many times because I thought that I wasn't gifted enough to accomplish what He was asking me to do.

> *Jesus almost never asks us to do*
> *things that are comfortable.*

Jesus told the man to pick up his bed, which was against the rules that the Jewish leaders and rabbis had established for observing the Sabbath. What Jesus was telling this man to do was not only counterintuitive, but also countercultural. Jesus will never ask you to do something that contradicts His Word, but He will certainly ask you to get uncomfortable! The man by the pool of Bethesda had the option to stay on his bed or respond to Jesus and rise. You have that same option. Don't get bogged down with trying to figure out everything in your mind before you take the first step. Instead of reasoning, respond and *rise*!

Rising requires us to move from a lower position to a higher position. If we want to rise, we need to stop procrastinating and start taking steps in the direction of our God-given dreams. No more hitting the snooze button on your life!

I love to sleep in, and I'm guilty of pressing the snooze button every ten minutes for an hour. When I think about rising, I think about how much I love that snooze button because it gives me permission to stay in bed for another ten minutes. My alarm feels more like an inconvenience than an invitation to get up and get moving.

Don't we all get like that sometimes in life? God is asking us to rise, but it's not convenient for us. It's a disruption of our cozy little lives. Instead of rising out of comfort or familiarity and into a life of purpose, we hit the snooze button, telling ourselves that we'll get around to it later. Sure, we want whatever it is that God is calling us to do and be, but not enough to move by faith. Like the man by the pool, we tell ourselves that we lack the means, but really we lack the motivation. If you truly want to rise and respond to God's Word, you have to let go of that mental snooze button. The time to rise isn't tomorrow; it's right now!

What Does Rising Look Like for You?

God may be telling you to call that person you have been avoiding, pray for a person randomly, apologize to your spouse, drop your work and spend time with your child, leave the ministry you have loved for so long and wait for new instructions, start a blog, share your story, or write a book. Whatever it is, if God is telling you to go, don't say "no." Rise and respond to the instructions God has placed on your heart before you have time to start talking yourself out of it.

Question: Is God calling you to start something new or recommit to something old? Is He calling you to leave a particular place or stop doing something? Is He calling you to go someplace new? What would rising look like for you?

_____

_____

_____

_____

_____

_____

Make no mistake, choosing to rise is a big step, but that doesn't necessarily mean that it will look big to other people. For example, God may be calling you to be a stay-at-home mom, but you are minimizing that call because our society doesn't magnify it as a worthwhile pursuit for a woman. You may think that focusing on raising your children instead of pursuing a career outside of the home means that you lack ambition or courage, even though you are doing exactly what God has called you to do.

We tend to think that if God is calling us to something, it has to be something that we and the world around us would consider big. As a result, we may end up minimizing what God has called us to do and miss out on the blessings of rising in our current season.

For some of us, rising looks like going for that dream that seems impossible. For some of us, rising means seeking help and counsel in the areas where we are holding on to the heaviness of pain so we can begin the process of healing. For some of us, rising is staying right where we are and being faithful with what is in front of us.

Question: What steps can you take to begin or continue to rise?

_____

_____

_____

_____

_____

_____

Embrace Your God-Given Authority

When Jesus spoke to the man, he somehow found the strength to stand up. For thirty-eight years, he had lacked the strength to get into the pool, but in that moment, he had the strength not only to pick up his bed, but to walk. This bed represented comfort, but also struggle, shame, and excuses. It held in it the story of thirty-eight years of bondage.

Jesus commanding this man to pick up his bed and walk reminds me of Genesis 4:7, in which God warned Cain that he needed to master the sin that was trying to control him: "If you do well, will you not be accepted? And if you do not do well, sin lies at the door. And its desire is for you, but you should rule over it" (NKJV). The man picking up his bed illustrates what God is saying in that verse. It's a visual representation of a person controlling the thing that once controlled him. Whatever bondage you may be suffering does not have to control you. God has given you authority over it and everything attached to it.

God has given you authority over your fears, your pain, your addictions, and your guilty pleasures. The only master you have in your life is the master you choose, so choose Christ. Choose freedom. Choose to live in your God-given authority by rising up, taking control of anything and everything that has held you captive, and moving forward.

As we discussed in Chapter Two, the spirit of fear is not from God. We have power over fear in Christ Jesus. In Galatians 4:6–7, Paul reminds us, "...because you are sons, God has sent forth the Spirit of His Son into your hearts, crying out, 'Abba, Father!' Therefore you are no longer a slave but a son, and if a son, then an heir of God through Christ" (NKJV).

Slaves are controlled by their masters. When you say that you are a child of God, you are proclaiming that neither fear nor any other form of slavery has any power over your life. You are proclaiming that God is the One who has authority over everything and that He has shared that authority with you as His child and heir. God has empowered you, so live in that power!

When we pick up our beds, it means that we have chosen to eliminate excuses and emerge from bondage. We have chosen to have faith and exercise our God-given authority over our lives. We can cultivate and strengthen our faith by studying the Bible, embracing God's truth in our lives, and taking steps of faith, however small they may be.

The Dangers of Comfort and Convenience

We all have our areas of comfort and familiarity. I know that I am certainly comfortable remaining comfortable. I don't naturally create space for myself to say "yes" to things that make me uncomfortable. For example, my husband is a very social person. His idea of a great day includes making connections and having conversations with all kinds of new people. That kind of day takes a lot of energy for me.

I'm an introvert, so a great day for me would be spent at the lake, reading my Bible or a book I enjoy, journaling, dreaming, and simply finding contentment in the stillness of nature. The last thing I want to do is go to a networking event. When my husband asks me to join him for an event like that, it takes a lot out of me to say "yes." But if I say "no," I miss the opportunity to support my husband and to step out of my comfort zone.

My fear of rejection encouraged me to stay in my comfort zone, but that comfort turned into isolation and social anxiety. Once I was able to move past that phase in my life, I started to realize that I had got comfortable in the dreaming phase, where all I did was think and write about the dreams and desires God has placed on my heart. Which is deceptive because I learned that solely dreaming can be mistaken for action. Sometimes we think that dreaming alone is enough, but if we aren't putting in the effort, it means that we're expecting a life of freedom and fulfillment to fall into our laps.

Dreaming is not the same as doing!

I had fun thinking and talking about what I would like to do, but I realized that I was merely standing on the sidelines, watching other people do things that God had also placed in my heart. I had become comfortable in my routine, and I didn't want to make the sacrifices necessary to make time for activities and pursuits that would engage my passions and bring joy to my heart. If an opportunity took me outside of my comfort zone or didn't fit into my daily routine, I would turn it down.

Every day, we're faced with opportunities to say "yes" to things that will take us out of our comfort zone. We may think that these opportunities aren't always connected to a greater purpose, but they are. Life offers us unexpected treasures that we won't discover if we don't say "yes" to trying something new, even if the opportunity doesn't initially seem worth our time and effort.

Being comfortable is a dangerous state of mind for Christians with dreams and Jesus followers who desire to experience the miraculous power of God in their lives. I'm not saying to forfeit contentment with what God has given you and where He has placed you. My point is that we shouldn't get so comfortable that we constantly choose the convenient option and miss out on all of the other possibilities that life has to offer.

Moses said "yes" to God's call to return to Egypt and lead God's people out of slavery, even though he didn't feel qualified (Exodus 3–4). Jeremiah said "yes" to God's call, even though he thought that he was too young (Jeremiah 1:6).

Abraham left his home to go to a place that God would show him (Genesis 12). Yes, the Bible says just that: "a land that I will show you" (Genesis 12:1 NKJV). God didn't even give Abraham a specific destination! Abraham left everything he knew because he was following a promise. He wasn't following proof; he was following a promise.

That's what we are all called to do. Faith is "evidence of things we cannot see" (Hebrews 11:1 NLT). My point is that I haven't discovered a calling in the Bible that was convenient. Every calling required faithful obedience and came with some level of discomfort and sacrifice.

Question: What are some areas in your life where you're settling for comfort and convenience?

_____

_____

_____

_____

_____

_____

What if the man by the pool of Bethesda had chosen to stay in his familiar, limited world? If he had given Jesus excuses or dismissed His instructions as impossible, his story would have been very different. He would probably have spent the rest of his life lying on that mat. If he had chosen not to respond to the very words of God and rise, he would never have known that he could walk. He would have stayed in bondage, having the ability to walk but not the faith to act.

Responding in faith to Jesus' words required the man to think and behave differently from how he thought and behaved for the past thirty-eight years. He had to use his mind and muscles in unfamiliar ways. He couldn't rise while continuing to do the same things he had done before. Ultimately, rising required him to exercise his faith and walk in his new ability, and that's also what is necessary for you and me to start moving forward. We have to be willing to change the way we think and the way we approach life, or our lives will never change. We have to exercise our faith and step forward into the unfamiliar. This is how we rise.

Your "I Was" Story

The man in John 5 didn't know who Jesus was. He addressed Jesus as "sir," and when the Jewish leaders asked him who had healed him, he had no name to give them (John 5:7, 11–13 NKJV). It wasn't until Jesus approached him at the temple that the man realized who had healed him (John 5:14–15).

In that moment, the man's testimony changed. He understood that he had been healed and freed from bondage by Jesus. The moment he got up and started walking, he had an "I was" story. He *was* the man who had been paralyzed for thirty-eight years, but now he was healed and walking in freedom because Jesus called him to rise.

This man's story could have continued without change. He could have been going on his thirty-ninth year of lying on his mat and making the same excuses. He could have continued to wait for help getting into the pool, but he didn't. He decided that he would follow the command of Jesus. He would take Jesus at His word and *rise*.

He went from waiting on an opportunity and help for thirty-eight years to being the man who chose to rise and begin walking. He became a man healed by Jesus, the Savior of the world. His courage to obey changed his infirmity into his testimony.

Rising means obeying God and doing what He is calling you to do. Taking a step toward the life you know you're capable of having gives you the opportunity to have an "I was" story.

I was the woman who allowed the fear of what other people might think of me to control me. I allowed fear to keep me from being obedient to God's voice. I allowed my own critical voice to control me as well. Then I decided to silence my fears by saying "yes" to Jesus and beginning the journey of investing the talents God has given me. Today I continue to face my fear by saying "yes" to God and the tasks He gives me that require me to pick up my mat and walk.

When we step out in faith, things change.
We change. We grow.

Whatever narrative you're giving yourself about why you can't move in the direction you really want to go will continue to control your life if you let it. So change the narrative by taking the hand you have been dealt and creating something beautiful out of it. God will bless what you give Him. He will take what you may consider to be not enough and do miracles with it!

Question: What do you want your "I was, but now I am" story to be?

_____

_____

_____

_____

_____

_____

Get Set! Go!

In this chapter, we discovered the power of being obedient to the P.U.R.P.O.S.E. to which God has called you:

1. Decide that you want to be made well. In every paralyzed area of your life, Jesus is calling you to walk with Him and explore uncharted territory.

2. Ask yourself the tough questions: Are you pursuing the things that God has placed in your heart? Are you actively facing your fears and taking advantage of opportunities outside of your comfort zone? Are you doing your part and trusting God with the rest? Recognize your excuses as excuses and come to terms with the issues that are preventing you from moving forward.

3. Rise and respond to the instructions God has placed on your heart before you have time to talk yourself out of it.

Moving from waiting to walking requires faith, and God can do something beautiful with every ounce of faith you have. If a mustard seed of faith can move mountains, if a bleeding woman can touch Jesus' clothes and be healed, if Jesus can feed five thousand people with only two fish and five loaves of bread, how much more will God use your faith and do beyond what you would ask or could even imagine?

It's time for you to rise in faith and walk in freedom.

Allow Jesus to give you your own "I was" story. All you have to do is pick up your bed and walk.

Chapter Six Notes

*Take some time to unpack all
your takeaways from this chapter*

_____

_____

_____

_____

_____

_____

_____

_____

_____

_____

_____

_____

_____

_____

Overcome the Obstacles

You taught my feet to dance upon disappointment
and I, I will worship.[11]

—Amanda Cook

Obstacles can be identified as the things that we believe are keeping us from moving forward in pursuit of the dreams that God has placed in our hearts. But what if we were to look at obstacles differently? What if we could overcome our obstacles by seeing them in a new light?

What if we were to see our
obstacles as opportunities?

Some obstacles are beyond our control, and some obstacles we create. Most of the time, you are your own biggest obstacle, and the only person stopping you from moving forward in life is *you*.

Obstacles can cause us to become discouraged and

keep us from pressing forward and staying the course. If God has placed a dream in your heart, I want to encourage you to press through the obstacles. Don't allow discouragement to distract you from the life God has for you.

You know the life I'm talking about, the life we can believe is possible for everyone else but struggle to believe for ourselves. We can see how amazing other individuals are and how God is working in their lives, but we have a hard time believing in our own capabilities. If you desperately want doors to open for you but are finding yourself stuck in a pool of discouragement, this chapter is for you.

The *O* in our P.U.R.P.O.S.E. acronym stands for "Overcome the obstacles." At the end of the day, the only thing we have control over is ourselves. We can't control other people. We can't always control the direction of our journey. We can't control when or if doors will open for us in the way that we hope. We can only control ourselves and how we respond to what happens as we continue our journey of living with P.U.R.P.O.S.E.

God has given us the strength and power to overcome obstacles, the ones that are beyond our control and the ones we create for ourselves. But what if we started to see obstacles as opportunities? Within every perceived obstacle is an experience from which we can gain purpose and perspective, and that makes all the difference.

Freedom from obstacles requires us to seek help. We need to recognize our bondage and say, *"It's not okay to stay here!"* We need to ask ourselves, *"What would it look like if I were free in this area?"* Then we need to seek

God, professional guidance, and accountability partners to help us overcome each obstacle and continue moving forward in our journey of purposeful living.

Don't Let Discouragement Define Your Response

Discouragement is one of the most common responses we have to the obstacles in our lives. The prefix in the word *discouragement* is *dis*, meaning "away from."[12] When you're discouraged, you're literally moved away from courage, strength, confidence, and enthusiasm.

One definition I found describes discouragement as "a loss of confidence or enthusiasm; dispiritedness."[13] The word *loss* in that definition indicates that before discouragement took over, you were enthusiastic, confident, and hopeful. Then something happened, and discouragement crept in and settled in your heart, causing you to lose the courage, enthusiasm, confidence, and hope that you once had regarding a specific matter.

Obstacles can become opportunities that help us to develop perspective and perseverance.

You might have lost these things, but that doesn't mean you can't find them again. You can learn to press through and stay the course, no matter what obstacles come your way.

Question: What is it about your journey that is bringing you the most discouragement?

_____

_____

_____

_____

_____

_____

I would like to introduce you to a woman who struggled with a seemingly impossible obstacle and had every reason to be discouraged, doubtful, and even defeated, yet she persevered and overcame. We find her story in Mark 5:25–32 (NKJV):

> Now a certain woman had a flow of blood for twelve years, and had suffered many things from many physicians. She had spent all that she had and was no better, but rather grew worse. When she heard about Jesus, she came behind Him in the crowd and touched His garment. For she said, "If only I may touch His clothes, I shall be made well."
>
> Immediately the fountain of her blood was dried up, and she felt in her body that she was healed of the affliction. And Jesus, immediately knowing in Himself that power had gone out of Him, turned around in the crowd and said, "Who touched My clothes?"

But His disciples said to Him, "You see the multitude thronging You, and You say, 'Who touched Me?'"

And He looked around to see her who had done this thing.

Put yourself in her shoes. You have been bleeding for twelve years, which has made you unclean that entire time according to Leviticus 15:19–33. Because you are unclean, you are an outcast, alienated from the rest of society. No one has touched you in twelve years. If you have children, you haven't been able to hold them because they can't touch you.

What a terrible thing to endure! This woman must have felt lonely, abandoned, and defeated. She spent all of her money seeking a cure for her medical condition, and the doctors who were supposed to help her only made things worse.

Here's the truth of the matter: you don't have to be struggling with an issue of blood to feel the emotions this woman felt. You don't have to have her exact condition to know what it's like to want something so badly but it always feels like it's out of reach.

Healing Comes in Different Forms

This woman suffered for twelve long years. The number twelve in the Bible carries the symbolic meaning of power and control.[14] I think it's safe to say that the issue of blood controlled every aspect of this woman's life, and

I believe that using the number twelve is another way God was highlighting the power this condition had over the woman.

Have you ever had a problem or condition that spilled into every area of your life and grieved your heart so deeply that you couldn't get it off your mind? Sometimes one aspect of our lives ends up controlling all of the other aspects, taking over our minds and dictating our actions. If we allow them to, fear and past trauma will hijack our actions, thoughts, and emotions and eventually take over our lives.

The most important part of this woman's story is her faith. Even though the issue of blood controlled this woman's life, she believed that Jesus had power over her medical condition. This is true for you, too. Whatever obstacle you're struggling with, whatever has taken control of your life, Jesus has power over it.

Nothing is bigger than Jesus! Maybe we have allowed an obstacle to become bigger than Jesus in our minds, but the truth is that it's not. Jesus has power over it, and you can be healed. I'm talking about all kinds of healing, not just physical healing.

Sometimes, however, healing doesn't look the way we expect it to look. For some of us, healing doesn't mean that our problem is completely resolved. It may mean that we are no longer held in bondage to it. Even if the condition or situation is still there, we have mental and emotional freedom from its control.

There are times when God heals us and grants us the desires of our hearts, and there are other times when healing comes in a different form. True freedom is being at peace even when the storms are raging around us.

It would have been so easy for this woman to respond to this long-standing obstacle with discouragement and lose all hope. But instead of giving up, she took an even greater risk by reaching out to Jesus for healing, or perhaps she felt that she had nothing left to lose. How did she do it? I have highlighted five aspects of the woman's inspiring response that we can apply to our lives as we work to overcome our own obstacles.

Pursue Your Freedom

First, the woman with the issue of blood pursued freedom in order to overcome her obstacle. Freedom truly is a pursuit. If we are in Christ Jesus, we are already free. But just as we need to seek God continually in order to know Him better, we also need to make sure that we are not allowing anything to encroach on our freedom. We need to make sure that the obstacles we face do not dictate the direction of our lives, and that requires taking action.

I once had the mindset that God would do everything for me. I just needed to believe in Him and wait for Him to make it happen. But if I want to take a bath, I can't sit there, waiting for the water to run. I have to turn on the faucet. Similarly, if I want to know God more, I can't sit there, waiting for Him to drop wisdom into my lap. I have to study His Word.

I don't know many people who are able to take baths and get clean without turning on the faucet, and I don't know many people who are able to have a profound relationship with God without actively seeking Him.

Likewise, if we desire freedom, we have to pursue it. We have a part to play in experiencing our freedom.

Recently, during a sweet time of worship and prayer, the Lord told me to speak to Him. He told me to tell Him what I wanted. I know that sounds so common. Shouldn't we always tell the Lord what we want? Isn't that part of the relationship we have with Him?

But I have to confess that the things I hold in my heart and allow to linger in my head don't always come out in prayer. I don't necessarily think to myself, *"I need to talk to God about that."* I usually try to figure out what to do on my own without ever taking it to the Lord. Oftentimes, it's not until I'm frustrated and at my wits' end that I realize I need God and start talking to Him.

When God asked me to tell Him what I wanted, I spoke to Him about the things I was worried about. I asked Him to help me be more patient in my marriage and stop getting so frustrated over the little things. I asked Him to take care of the results of the women's conference I was planning, wondering if anyone would show up. I confessed that I was struggling with feelings of inadequacy and asked Him for encouragement.

As I talked to God about what I was feeling throughout the day, He began to reveal to me that I needed to start thanking Him. He showed me that I was praying for things that were already in my possession. When I thank Him, I remember that I already have a firm grasp on my greatest desire: His promises. Therefore, I try to remind myself not only to have prayers of petitions and repentance, but to cultivate a prayer life based on praising and thanking God.

I have also become more intentional about praying in

ways that help me to refocus on God's promises found in Scripture. For example, I thank Him that I can be strong and courageous because He goes with me and will never leave me or forsake me (Deuteronomy 31:6). I thank Him that He has equipped me with everything I need to do His will and that He is always at work in my life (Hebrews 13:20–21).

As I have stated before, this book was a result of me wanting to be free from my fear of other people's judgment. I sought God in this area, and this book came from my personal pursuit of freedom. I also want to have whole and healthy relationships. In addition to studying God's Word and taking risks in friendships, I have sought counseling. You have to be intentional if you want to live in freedom.

Question: I encourage you to take some time to sit with the Lord and talk to Him about the things that are consuming your mind and heart. Write those things down on the lines below. What is one thing you can do to begin pursuing healing and freedom in each of these areas?

_____

_____

_____

_____

_____

_____

Question: What promises from Scripture can you confess over these things?

_____

_____

_____

_____

_____

_____

Question: How can you thank God in light of these promises from Scripture?

_____

_____

_____

_____

_____

This is a practice that will take time and commitment, but if you follow it on a regular basis, you will gain a new perspective on your obstacles and start to experience freedom in every area of your life. Confess God's promises over the fears and problems that have been controlling your mind and heart. When you learn to focus on thanking Him, you will notice a shift. Then you will find the hope you need to walk out of the pit of discouragement and into brighter days of victory!

Take Initiative

Second, the woman with the issue of blood *took initiative* to overcome her obstacle. She knew what she wanted, and she went after it. She didn't wait for the perfect time or the perfect situation. She saw the opportunity to receive healing from Jesus, and she took it. This woman could have made all kinds of excuses: *"It's much too crowded. I'll never be able to get close enough to Him. There's no way He will be able to heal me. I've already tried everything. It's too late."* She could easily have allowed hopelessness to take over and let the moment pass, but she didn't.

Some of us feel like we have to have everything together before we take initiative, but the truth is that sometimes we need to put things out there even if they're not perfect. Sometimes we need to go for something when we don't have all of the answers and all we have in front of us is an opportunity.

This doesn't mean that we shouldn't do our best or that we should be lazy about the details. Having a plan is great, and we should do everything we can to make ourselves or our product ready before we put it out there. However, if you are a creative person who always strives to do your best, you will always look at your work with a critical eye and think about all of the ways it could be better.

We have the choice to take what we believe is our very best and put it out there or wait until the day when we think that it's perfect. The problem with choosing to wait for perfection is that we may never get there. The problem with waiting for the perfect time is that it may never come.

You may have to create the perfect time by making a choice to plunge ahead. If we don't seize opportunities and create them, we will look up and realize that five or ten years have passed with no progress. Taking initiative means being willing to start somewhere.

> **Question:** Have you been working on something that you're hesitant to put out there? In what ways might perfectionism be keeping you from taking initiative?

> _____

> _____

> _____

> _____

> _____

> _____

There have been times when I have felt discouraged and stuck because I didn't see things happening in my life that I really wanted to happen. Many times, those feelings were rooted in the fact that I wasn't taking initiative and working toward the outcomes I desired.

The whole concept of taking initiative makes me think of when Jesus fed the five thousand (Matthew 14:13–21). The disciples thought that the people should be dismissed to go buy food for themselves. Like many of us, they had excuses about not having enough time or resources. It was getting late, and they were in a remote place (Matthew

14:15). They looked at what they had to offer, five loaves of bread and two fish, and said that it wasn't enough (Matthew 14:17). Haven't you seen yourself in a similar light, feeling that what you had to offer wasn't adequate?

But Jesus wasn't asking His disciples for what they did not have; He wanted what they already possessed. He took those five loaves of bread and two fish and did something supernatural with them. It takes faith to give Jesus what you have, especially when you don't think that it's enough.

When you give Jesus what you have— your time, your resources, and your talents—you give Him the opportunity to do something supernatural with it.

Don't worry about the time or resources you don't have. Take initiative by starting with what you know and offering what you have. Then watch Jesus do something supernatural with it!

Question: What do you perceive as a limitation in your life? Is it time, resources, inadequacy, or lack of knowledge or experience? How can you use what you already have to bless someone else?

_____

_____

_____

_____

_____

_____

Be Courageous and Take Risks

Third, the woman with the issue of blood took a risk when she saw an opportunity. When I think about risk, I envision the word *love*. We all have the desire to love and be loved, but to love others and be loved in return, we have to take risks.

Every relationship requires risk.

Can I trust this person? Will this person keep my secrets and cherish my time? Will he or she protect my heart or choose to abandon me when my flaws are revealed?

When we meet new people and start to develop new relationships, we don't know the answers to those questions. We don't know if other people will truly honor our secrets or if they will head for the hills when they find out that we have a somewhat crazy side. The only way we will ever experience love is if we move forward and risk the pain and disappointment of a failed relationship.

Life offers the same thing. We will never know what's on the other side of comfort or fear if we don't plunge ahead and take a leap of faith. When we stay comfortable and avoid taking risks, we rob ourselves of the opportunity to acquire wisdom, which is one of life's most valuable gifts. On the other hand, when we step out in obedience and take risks, we gain priceless wisdom and intimacy with Jesus. Out there in the place of faith and risk is where life transformation happens.

This woman's healing came in response to the risk she took. Remember Leviticus 15:19–33. Because of her bleeding condition, she was considered unclean and forbidden to participate in society. Staying as she was would have resulted in continued misery, isolation, and suffering.

This is where the big question comes in: Do we take the risk and believe that the outcome will be great gain, or do we shrink back in fear, thinking of all the reasons we shouldn't take a leap of faith? Often we remain stagnant because we're focusing solely on the possibility of loss and the pain it would cause. In order to have the courage to take initiative and take risks, we need to fix our eyes on what we could gain, not what we might lose. That's what this woman did. She fixed her eyes on the prize: Jesus, the One who could heal her.

> *Courage is taking a step of faith, not really knowing if what you want to happen will materialize.*

In my early twenties, I took over the homeless ministry for my church. Several of the members had rooted for me to step in and become their leader. I gracefully accepted and took the lead. I felt that God had given me a vision that we would have several church services and Bible studies all throughout San Diego. When I shared this vision, several people were on board.

Two of my friends and ministry partners took the plunge with me and said, "We are with you. Let's do it." Another group had a different vision. They wanted to create a shelter for the homeless and believed that should be our ministry focus. It was a great idea, but I felt that the timing was not right and the idea lacked the commitment it needed to thrive. I had to have the courage to tell them that I couldn't move forward with their vision. I gave them the option to move forward with the vision I had in place or to separate from the ministry and begin their own ministry.

It was a difficult decision to make. I didn't know if what I envisioned would happen. I hoped that it would. I told everyone in our ministry that's where we were headed, but I had doubts of my own, many of them. What if I was wrong? Was I a bad leader? I didn't have any real leadership experience prior to leading the homeless ministry. What if building a home for the homeless was the direction we should have taken? Should I have focused on a shelter before pursuing evangelistic efforts? Was I making the right decision? Those questions haunted me for a while.

I was thankful that I had friends who took the baton and ran with it. I had leaders who believed in me and the vision when I doubted. I'm not sure if they know it, but I borrowed their faith many times. Their faith was a catalyst in helping me to become a better leader.

We had about twenty committed volunteers, and of the

twenty, I had two leaders who believed in the vision and led the ministry with me. That was all I needed. Who would have thought I only needed two, not twenty?

Over the course of several years, we saw ministries evolving all over San Diego, just as I had envisioned. My ministry partners and friends now had leaders under them, and God was allowing our ministry to thrive. It was and still is one of the most treasured ministry experiences of my lifetime.

Not all of my visions end so well, but this one was a courageous risk that paid off. I believed that my vision would become a reality, but I wasn't completely sure. Living courageously means not knowing for sure what the outcome will be. That's what makes it a risk. You're not sure that what you desire to happen will happen, but you take the chance. Looking back, you will realize that taking the risk gave you a priceless gift that you wouldn't have experienced if you hadn't gone for it: the opportunity to do what you have never done, become who you knew you could become, and experience what you have never had but always wanted. Friend, dare to live courageously by taking risks.

Question: Are you afraid to take a risk that might help you to overcome an obstacle in your life? What is it about that risk that intimidates you?

_____

_____

_____

_____

_____

_____

Question: What are the possible gains for you and others if you were to go for it?

_____

_____

_____

_____

_____

I believe that this woman who had suffered for so long was focused on what she could gain, not what she could lose. Her example might be the inspiration you need to move forward and take more risks in life. Don't allow fear, comfort, or discouragement to rob you of a blessing that God has for you. This woman had every reason to feel afraid and discouraged, but she didn't let that stop her. She had faith to believe in the possibilities. Do you?

Stay Focused on the Right Thing

Fourth, the woman with the issue of blood stayed focused on the right thing in order to overcome her obstacle. Doing so helped her to navigate through the crowd and get close to Jesus. She wanted healing, and she was focused on Jesus because she believed that He was the source of healing.

For this woman to touch Jesus, she had to push through the crowd, and this is true for us as well. It may be a crowd of our own doubts, defeats, and fears or a crowd of naysayers who don't believe in our dreams. Once we start taking steps forward in obedience, moving in the direction we believe God is calling us, we often experience a setback. We start off excited, but then our sense of purpose gets swallowed by the crowd of life's distractions, disappointments, and defeats. Caught up in life's demands and detours, we put our God-directed pursuits on the back burner. Sometimes it's not that we're confused about what God is calling us to do; we're just doubtful about how it's going to happen.

If you don't want your dreams to be trampled by the crowd, you have to keep your eyes fixed on Jesus. You have to persevere and push through to Him. That's what this woman did, and it gave her courage and faith. She kept her eyes on Jesus as she was pursuing what she desired with all of her heart.

Question: What in your life is crowding out your pursuit of the dreams God has placed in your heart? Is it limiting or false beliefs, your fears and insecurities, your past defeats, your busy schedule, or naysayers around you?

_____

_____

_____

_____

_____

_____

This section is about recognizing everything that's keeping you from fixing your eyes on Jesus, every distraction and detour. Identifying what you have been focusing on will give you the wisdom to start moving in the direction of faith.

Fix your eyes on Jesus. He will give you vision, faith, and courage and help you to press through the crowd. In order to fix your eyes on Jesus as you keep taking steps of faith, you need to create space in your life to connect with Him regularly and bring Him into everything you do.

How do I keep my feet on the ground and my eyes on Jesus? Almost every day, I find time to replenish my soul by reading my Bible or a devotional, writing in my journal, or going for a walk. I sit down and envision my dreams, and then I make a deliberate plan for taking initiative in my "life work." I find inspirational quotations and Bible verses, and I write them down on small pieces of paper. I post these positive notes where I will see them throughout my day to keep me motivated and inspired to take one step at a time. I also work on my personal development by reading books that challenge my way of thinking and equip me to move forward with becoming all that God created me to be.

Speak Words of Faith!

Lastly, the woman with the issue of blood spoke words of faith to get to what she wanted: proximity to Jesus and healing. "If only I may touch His clothes, I shall be made well" (Mark 5:28 NKJV), she told herself as she pressed through the crowd to touch Jesus. This is by far one of my favorite parts of the story.

I envision this crowd being loud and aggressive, like a crowd of shoppers on Black Friday. Instead of running toward discounted merchandise, they were running toward Jesus. This woman was in the thick of that crowd, speaking words of faith. She believed that Jesus had the power to make her whole. If she was going to be free, she believed that Jesus would be the one to free her.

Please don't misunderstand. This message is not about speaking certain words to create the reality of your choice. It's not a matter of hocus-pocus, saying the right words so that what you want will magically appear. Yes, our words have power, but my point is that you need to be aware of the narrative you're creating in your mind. The words in our minds, whether we speak them out loud or not, reveal what's in our hearts.

This woman believed in her heart that if she could just touch Jesus, she would be healed. One significant attribute we find in the woman is her faith, but I also believe that her faith birthed something pivotal that we can learn from: expectation. She expected that Jesus would do what only

He could do and no one else could. She pressed through the crowd with great expectation of our Savior.

We need to have faith that births expectation. We can expect our God to do what only He can do in our lives. We can expect Him to do miracles. He is the One who parted the Red Sea, fed the multitudes, restored sight, and raised the dead. He heals, He speaks, He calls, He provides, and He equips. May the words you think and speak proclaim His truth and promises over your life. You can expect great things from God. He gives good and perfect gifts.

Imagine your mother telling you that she has a gift for you under a tree, but under the tree, there are several gifts for other people as well. You look at the tree and realize that there are a ton of gifts, but you know that there is one with your name on it because your mom told you that there was a gift for you. You walk over to the tree, expecting to find in your gift box the keys to your very first home, the home you have been praying and waiting for. You're so excited. You look at several boxes and don't see your name, but you don't give up. You keep looking for the gift that has your name on it because you know that it's there. How do you know? Because your mother told you so. Finally, after a long search, you find the box with your name on it. You open the gift, and it's the keys to your very first home, just as you had hoped. Aren't you glad that you didn't give up?

In the same way, God has gifts for us in the form of His promises. We can expect these gifts in our lives because He has given them to us in His Word. We may have to search through a few boxes to get there, but holding His gift in our hands is possible. Whatever promise you are waiting to see come to pass, you can expect that Jesus will do what He said He would do. You can walk into every day, knowing that God has a gift with your name on it. Stay expectant. Continue looking. Keep speaking words of faith.

Question: What words have been in your mind and coming out of your mouth? Are they words of fear or words of faith?

_____

_____

_____

_____

_____

Question: What if you were to wake up every day with expectation of God's best for your life? How do you think it would change the words you speak? What are you expecting by faith that Jesus will do in your life?

_____

_____

_____

_____

_____

As you move in the direction you believe God is calling you, I want you to listen to the conversations you have with yourself and the words that are coming out of your mouth. Evaluate your expectations. If they're not helping you to overcome your obstacles by seeing opportunities, you need to change them. Choose your words wisely.

You Can Control Your Response

When we're faced with an obstacle, our response is very important. The example of the woman with the issue of blood teaches us to resist staying in discouragement and instead to respond to the obstacles in our lives by pursuing our freedom, taking initiative, taking risks, staying focused on Jesus, and speaking words of faith.

Question: Of the five responses to obstacles, which one speaks to you the most regarding your current season? Why?

_____

_____

_____

_____

_____

_____

Question: What life changes do you need to make to start exercising your faith and living with expectation? Choose one specific change and break it down into manageable steps you can start taking today.

_____

_____

_____

_____

_____

_____

Obstacles are opportunities for growth. When I look at an obstacle, I try to think about all of the possibilities of what God can do with it and what I can do with it. I got kicked off my track team in college for making poor decisions. I thought that my career was over. I thought that I had failed. I used that time to continue training and earn my place back on the team, and I learned that one poor decision can cost you everything. I learned from that obstacle and applied the lessons to my everyday life.

Some obstacles are ones that I create. I never saw myself writing a book. I looked at all of the challenges of writing a book. I saw all of the amazing books and teachers out there and convinced myself that there wasn't any room for me. There were already good teachers.

Then I took the obstacle I had created and made it an opportunity to do what I admire others doing while adding my own twist, my unique fingerprint. No one else has my testimony. No one can dream my dream better than I can.

Now I use that as my fuel to persevere. There is no obstacle too high or too big that a mustard seed of faith cannot move it.

Get Set! Go!

In this chapter, we looked at how to overcome the obstacles to living with P.U.R.P.O.S.E.:

1. Pursue your freedom. Don't let discouragement define your responses.
2. When you see an opportunity, don't shrink back. Take initiative and take the risk! Stay focused on what you can gain, not what you might lose. Fix your eyes on Jesus and speak words of faith. Trust God to turn obstacles into opportunities!

You can't always control what obstacles you will face or when they will appear, but you can control your response. You can overcome every obstacle by finding the opportunity that lies within it. I'll say it again: you can!

Chapter Seven Notes

*Take some time to unpack all
your takeaways from this chapter*

_____

_____

_____

_____

_____

_____

_____

_____

_____

_____

_____

_____

_____

_____

Serve Well

Whatever your hand finds to do, do it with all your might…

—Ecclesiastes 9:10 (NIV)

We all desire to live a significant life and become all that we are created to be. We want to thrive. We want to be seen and heard. We want to know that we are valuable. At the very core, we have a desire for our lives to make a difference. Legacy means something to us. Making the world better for humanity matters to us. In my life, when I have seen, encountered, and experienced greatness, it has always been in the presence of great love poured out in acts of service.

The *S* in our P.U.R.P.O.S.E. acronym stands for "Serve well." To serve well, we need to be intentional about serving others and having an extraordinary work ethic. Serving well is not about what you obtain; it's about what you give!

Serve Well by Contributing Your Gifts

Having then gifts differing according to the grace that is given to us, let us use them: if prophecy, let us prophesy in proportion to our faith; or ministry, let us use it in our ministering; he who teaches, in teaching; he who exhorts, in exhortation; he who gives, with liberality; he who leads, with diligence; he who shows mercy, with cheerfulness.
—Romans 12:6–8 (NKJV)

Our gifts come from God. A gift is a talent or ability that God has given us. The purpose of our gifts is revealed in 1 Corinthians 12:7: "A spiritual gift is given to each of us so we can help each other" (NLT). God has given you a gift so that you can help other people.

You will know that you are using your gifts if you and the people you are serving experience God in profound ways as a result of your service. For example, when I am teaching, I experience God in new ways, and God has touched people and changed their lives through my teaching in ways that only He could. If we are going to serve well by contributing our gifts to the lives of others, we can boldly expect that people will profit from it, particularly fellow members of the body of Christ.

There are many different gifts, and I believe that serving the church body in any capacity, small or large, will help you to learn what your gifts are. Don't limit God to any type of personality test. Listen to His prompting in your heart more than anything else. God has ways of surprising us with gifts that we didn't know we had and perhaps didn't even know we wanted.

Serving others with your gifts requires walking with Jesus and leaning into Him so that He can equip you with the tools you need to help build up His Church. If you see a need and you have the ability to meet it, do it. In these moments, you have the opportunity to die to yourself, setting aside your discomfort, doubt, and inconvenience, and share the love of Jesus with others by serving them.

Question: Take some time to reflect on the different kinds of talents you may possess. Which gifts do you see evidence of in your life?

_____

_____

_____

_____

_____

_____

Question: In what ways can you begin to contribute your gifts for the benefit of others?

_____

_____

_____

_____

_____

_____

Question: If you don't know where to start, start with serving. Where can you begin serving other people? Will you invite people to your home? Will you start a small group? Will you get involved in a ministry at a local church? Will you serve meals?

_____

_____

_____

_____

_____

_____

A healthier family, a better community, and a better world may seem like daydreams, but they can become reality, and it all begins with our actions.

The passion and potential that God places within us are so much bigger than our fears.

One of my favorite quotations is from Erma Bombeck, and it goes like this: "When I stand before God at the end of my life, I would hope that I would not have a single bit of talent left, and could say, 'I used everything you gave me.'"[15] I hope we can all say that!

What would the world look like if you were to step up and step out into your calling? What if you were to write that book, and it changed the life of a person who read it? What if you were to share your story, and it gave someone hope?

Question: Think about the gifts God has given you and the dreams He has placed in your heart. What changes might you see in your family, your community, and the world if you were to step into your calling and serve the people around you?

_____

_____

_____

_____

_____

We Can't Serve Well When We're Comparing Ourselves

Before we get into the heart of what it means to serve well, let's get one thing straight: we will not be able to serve others if we are too busy comparing ourselves to them. What if someone else has the same gift or talent as you have? This can lead you to think that there isn't any room for you because there are so many other people already doing what you can do, just as well as or better than you can do it.

That's a limiting belief that will keep you from doing what you are meant to do in life. God only made one of you. No one will do what you do in the exact same way you do it. Whatever it is that you do, know that it will have your own unique fingerprint. There are several amazing preachers, but each one of them brings something different to the body of Christ. All of them are necessary. A gift will manifest itself differently in each person who possesses it.

> *There is no one else on this planet or*
> *in history who is exactly like you.*

Since God made you different from everyone else, there is room for your business idea, your ministry, your creativity, your teaching. Let me say it again: your work will have your unique fingerprint. Other people may be doing similar work, but your contribution is still essential and irreplaceable.

God's anointing on you is His appointing of you. He anoints and appoints each person according to the unique contribution that he or she can make. If God is the One who works through our differences, we can trust that He will guide us in the use of our gifts and take us into the right ministry and activities. Let me clarify what I mean by ministry. Ministry doesn't have to be in the church. Your ministry is where you choose to plant your feet and where you invest your gifts and talents with every ounce of your being. It can be your job, your home, or a role in your community.

It's important to stay connected with God in every aspect of our lives because He truly is in everything. He is the expert who can help us to navigate our gifts, our ministry, and our activities. When we operate in His Spirit rather than in our personal agenda, we glorify God.

God doesn't *need* us to use our gifts; He *wants* us to use our gifts! He invites us into His work. He equips us and gives us free will to choose to love Him and serve Him. We don't have to do anything for God, because God can do everything without us. We *get* to do the work He calls us to do. It's a blessing and a privilege! What a great feeling to know that He chooses us not because He needs us, but because He loves us and wants us to participate with Him. We can enter into every work He places in our hands and say, *"Not only do I get to do this, but I am empowered to do this!"*

If you truly want to bring God glory and participate in fulfilling His purposes, you won't accomplish it by sitting on the sidelines. You won't accomplish it by scrolling through social media, watching what other people are doing, and comparing yourself to them. You will accomplish it by confronting your insecurities, doing things that are uncomfortable and intimidating, taking risks, and loving people courageously.

If we want to live the life God has for us, there's no way around the uncomfortable.

We need to decide that it's time to press through the uncomfortable feeling instead of waiting for it to go away.

Our human minds are wired to keep us safe, so the moment our brains realize that we're going into uncharted territory, the safety alert goes off. Then our fear tries to talk us out of taking the risk.

We need to pray for peace in the midst of our discomfort, asking that God would settle our hearts and minds if He really does want us to do the uncomfortable thing we feel called to do. Sometimes our lack of peace is really fear trying to convince us that what God is asking us to do isn't safe. In those moments, it's easy to shrink back, convince yourself that the dream is too big, and disqualify yourself by talking yourself out of it.

My tendency was to think about all of the people who could do it better and had the time and resources that I didn't have. Then I chalked it up as impossible and went on with my day-to-day activities. I know what it's like to put my God-given dreams on the back burner, and I don't want that for you.

On the other hand, I also know what it's like to take that first step of faith in the direction of my passion and let me tell you, it is liberating! So, sis, claim and proclaim the value God has placed on your life and accept and embrace the value God has put on the lives of others. Stop comparing yourself to others and sitting on the sidelines. Bring your A game to everything you do, knowing that no one else can bring exactly what you have to offer. This is how you will begin to serve extraordinarily well.

Serving Well Means Knowing
Everyone Matters

Serving well requires us to understand how every part of the body of Christ matters—every talent, every gift, every area of service, every personality. Paul explained this in 1 Corinthians 12:12–27 (NLT), using the human body as an analogy:

The human body has many parts, but the many parts make up one whole body. So it is with the body of Christ. Some of us are Jews, some are Gentiles, some are slaves, and some are free. But we have all been baptized into one body by one Spirit, and we all share the same Spirit.

Yes, the body has many different parts, not just one part. If the foot says, "I am not a part of the body because I am not a hand," that does not make it any less a part of the body. And if the ear says, "I am not part of the body because I am not an eye," would that make it any less a part of the body? If the whole body were an eye, how would you hear? Or if your whole body were an ear, how would you smell anything?

But our bodies have many parts, and God has put each part just where he wants it. How strange a body would be if it had only one part! Yes, there are many parts, but only one body. The eye can never say to the hand, "I don't need you." The head can't say to the feet, "I don't need you."

In fact, some parts of the body that seem weakest and least important are actually the most necessary. And the parts we regard as less honorable are those we clothe with the greatest care. So we carefully protect those parts that should not be seen, while the more honorable parts do not require this special care. So God has put the body together such that extra honor and care are given to those parts that have less dignity. This makes for harmony among the members, so that all the members care for each other. If one part suffers, all the parts suffer with it, and if one part is honored, all the parts are glad.

All of you together are Christ's body, and each of you is a part of it.

Every part of the human body plays a significant role in our overall well-being. Every part of the body is needed for the body to function at its very best. The same is true of humankind; we need each other in order to thrive.

Just as every part of the body matters, every person matters. Everyone is valuable, and that includes you! This should encourage us to help each other live our best possible lives because when we all thrive, we all benefit.

Sometimes our selfishness gets in the way. When we want to be significant and get what we want, we focus on our own potential and what we need to do to reach the next level. We stop focusing on other people and their potential because we feel threatened and insecure. We're afraid that other people shining will somehow diminish our own light.

We need to let go of that mindset. Comparison is one

of the biggest tools that the enemy uses to distract us from what God is doing in our lives. We need to embrace a new mindset that empowers and encourages us and other people. Paul's analogy reminds us that everyone is valuable. Each of us has a place and a purpose.

It may take time and some trial and error to figure out where you fit in the body. Maybe you're trying to be a hand or an ankle, but things aren't working out because you're actually a nose. You could be trying to fit into a place that God did not intend for you. Can you imagine if our hands were in a different place? What if our hands were trying to act like feet? Continue to seek the Lord regarding your spiritual gifts and how you fit into the body, and He will guide you where He wants you.

Since every part is significant, regardless of its function, we can live confidently and focus on using the gifts God has given us to serve well. We don't have to waste our time and energy coveting what someone else has. We can have confidence in knowing that we, too, were meant to thrive. We can trust God's perfect plan for us, even when it looks different from someone else's life.

We may see the role of a janitor as less important than the role of a CEO, but imagine how much a company would suffer if the janitor didn't do his job properly. Having to work in a dirty office with filthy restrooms and bug and mold problems could certainly hinder the productivity of the CEO and everyone else in the office.

One of the greatest servants of the Lord I have ever met was named John. He worked at the discipleship school where my husband and I met. He wasn't one of the teachers. He was someone who took care of the needs of the school, making sure that the bathrooms were clean, the kitchen was tidy, and the people were prayed over. He always had a smile on his face and joy in his heart.

John's life and his willingness to serve well taught me so much. I learned that it's important to find your fit in your current season and embrace it wholeheartedly. I learned that serving with love is the most fulfilling way to serve. Some seasons render different gifts, and God gives us what we need for each situation. Whatever role you have and whatever season you may be in, know that you will serve well if you serve with excellence, have the right motives, and walk in love.

Care for Each Part of the Body

Serving well also means treating other people well. Let's revisit 1 Corinthians 12:25–27 (NLT):

> *This makes for harmony among the members, so that all the members care for each other. If one part suffers, all the parts suffer with it, and if one part is honored, all the parts are glad.*
>
> *All of you together are Christ's body, and each of you is a part of it.*

***We are called to celebrate and
to suffer with other people.***

Recognizing that we are all part of the same body should cause us to consider how to love people with compassion and empathy. I have heard the saying, "When you hurt someone else, you're also hurting yourself," but I didn't really understand what it meant until I read this Scripture passage. I have dropped things on my foot on more than one occasion, and I felt that pain in my entire body!

When we hurt someone else, we are also affected. When someone else in the body of Christ is in pain, we should meet that pain with compassion. We should strive to heal the body instead of hurting it. We should want other people to be better because we function at our best when all parts of the body are healthy and thriving.

When you hurt someone else, take responsibility and take initiative in helping that person to heal. You can't control how someone else will respond, but you can apologize, ask for forgiveness, and forgive. Serving well means doing your best to live at peace with yourself and others.

Question: Take some time to consider your relationships in the body of Christ. Are they healthy? If not, is there something you can do on your part to heal an unhealthy relationship?

_____

_____

_____

_____

_____

_____

Serving Well Means Working to Excel

To serve well, we need to put our all into whatever it is that our hands find to do. In other words, put your best effort forward. I believe in the saying, "Do your best, and God will cover the rest!" Let's revisit Romans 12:6–8, this time in the New Living Translation (NLT):

> *In his grace, God has given us different gifts for doing certain things well. So if God has given you the ability to prophesy, speak out with as much faith as God has given you. If your gift is serving others, serve them well. If you are a teacher, teach well. If your gift is to encourage others, be encouraging. If it is giving, give generously. If God has given you leadership ability, take the responsibility seriously. And if you have a gift for showing kindness to others, do it gladly.*

This Scripture passage is one of my absolute favorites. It's practical and tangible and doesn't require extensive theological knowledge to understand. We can read it just as it's written and apply it directly to our lives.

As children of God, we are not called to work with a mindset of mediocrity. We are called to excel in the things we do by doing the best we can. Whatever it is that you are doing, do it to the very best of your ability, even if you're not in the role you want to be in just yet.

Habits are powerful, and building high-performance habits in one area will transfer into everything else you do. If you start where you are, then when you get that dream job or dream opportunity, you will already have the work habits you need to excel. There's a scripture that runs through my mind frequently as a mantra: "Whatever your hand finds to do, do it with all your might" (Ecclesiastes 9:10 NIV). This scripture always reminds me to put my best effort forward in all that I do.

Question: Is there anything in your life to which you are not giving your best? Are there things that you're not doing with excellence? Why do you think that is?

_____

_____

_____

_____

_____

_____

You can be honest with yourself here, without condemnation or judgment. This is about having a starting point so you can work toward creating new habits to change the things you have the power to change. Sometimes we're not able to excel in the things we really want to excel in because we're stretched too thin. If that's the case for you, then taking things off your plate or delegating some of your responsibilities may be necessary. Sometimes we get sucked into the demands of life, and the things that we really want to give our best to end up getting less of our attention and energy. The real question is this: What do you need to do in order to serve well? Only you can answer that.

Serve Well by Being Brave

Being brave is about saying "yes" to the things we know in our hearts we're supposed to say "yes" to, instead of "no" or "not right now." When we focus on our fears and insecurities, they can become so big in our minds that it becomes hard to see a favorable outcome. But when we focus on God and other people, it stirs courage in our hearts, and we start to move in the direction God is calling us. Even when we're afraid, we find a little more freedom and courage with each step of faith we take. Keep your feet moving forward and your eyes looking up!

I don't speak much about the enemy—not because he isn't real, but because I know that he has no real power over God's authority. The Bible describes the devil as a "thief [who] comes only to steal and kill and destroy" (John 10:10 NIV). I want you to consider how powerful and impactful you would be if you were contributing and thriving in your gifts. How much of a threat to the enemy would you be if you were using your gifts to set people free from his lies and their own?

How different would your life be if you were living to serve others?

If you are contributing and thriving in your gifts, you will become a major threat to the enemy. So, child of God, be brave enough to renounce confusion and declare clarity over what God has given you. Renounce discouragement and declare that God can do something amazing and supernatural with your doubts, fears, and insecurities if you will just take a step of faith in the areas where He is calling you to grow and thrive.

Be brave enough to believe that God gave you a gift to offer to His people. Be brave enough to believe that there is room and need for your unique contribution. Be brave enough to face your demons and the lies you have been believing so that you can walk in the truth. You matter, and so does your gifting.

God has given us gifts so that we can make this world better by making the people in it better. If we choose not to use our gifts, whether intentionally or unintentionally, we are doing Him a disservice.

For years, I allowed my perception of time to keep me from serving others. I like to be comfortable, and serving Jesus by serving other people isn't comfortable. To this day, I still have to examine my heart and make sure that I'm not saying "no" to Jesus for the sake of being comfortable in my routine, doing my own thing with my family in my home.

Question: Being comfortable kept me from being brave. Is there anything keeping you from being brave? Are you choosing comfort over your calling?

_____

_____

_____

_____

_____

Take what is keeping you from being brave and surrender it to Jesus in prayer. Then it's time to do the hard thing and make the daily choice to step out of your comfort zone with bravery and intention.

Something that helps me to move forward with Jesus is examining my heart daily, and that naturally happens as a result of spending time with Him in the Word and writing in my journal. In addition, I am someone who likes a to-do list. I have to have a plan for my day. I incorporate items into my to-do list that will take me out of my comfort zone and require me to be brave, and then I actually do them! For example, I might make a note to contact an organization to see how our church or small group could serve there, or I might schedule time to call someone who has been on my heart to see how he or she is doing. I might make a plan to start studying a particular book of the Bible.

Being brave is an intentional choice.

The things that we really want to happen won't just happen. We need to discipline ourselves to examine our hearts and move forward in doing the hard things.

Serving Well: An Action Plan

Now that you have learned about gifts and what it looks like to serve well, how can you transform your knowledge into action? What practical steps can you take to serve well where God has you right now? I have identified six steps you can take to begin living out everything we have discussed in this chapter.

Action Step One: Make Your Family a Priority

I truly try to be intentional about making God my first priority, and my family is a close second. My life isn't perfect, and I don't get this right all of the time, but I certainly put effort into attaining this goal.

My husband and I were once asked to lead a mission trip, but we were told that the team would only be able to meet on Saturdays. That was a deal-breaker for us. Saturday was a day that I reserved just for my family. At that time, my husband was leading a young-adult ministry, and so much of his time was going into ministry functions. I felt that I needed to protect our time with each other because Sunday through Friday was given to ministry obligations. As much as we wanted to serve in

192 · ESTREANDA YATES

this capacity, we knew that it wasn't worth sacrificing our time together.

We declined the opportunity. A few days later, we received a call informing us that the team meetings could take place on another day of the week. We accepted the offer and planned our very first mission trip together. It was an amazing experience, one that we will forever treasure in our hearts.

There are so many things that will try to pull you away from your priorities. You need to keep in mind what is most important to you so that you will know when it's time to say "no." When we say "yes" to one thing, we are saying "no" to something else. When my husband and I said "no" to leading the mission trip, we were saying "yes" to continuing to build and nurture our relationship. In the end, we were able to do both, and I strongly believe that it was because we honored our commitment to one another and didn't compromise our time with each other that we saw God's favor upon us.

Yes, we had an opportunity to use our gifts and engage in work that we were truly passionate about, but it wasn't more important than nurturing our relationship with each other. As you move forward into a life of purpose, intentionally prioritize what's truly important to you by creating healthy boundaries so you can say "yes" to the things and the people that mean the most to you.

Question: Do you need to establish boundaries to protect your most valuable possession: family? Is there something you need to say "no" to so that you can say "yes" to the people who mean the most to you?

_____

_____

_____

_____

_____

_____

Action Step Two: Ask for Help and Plan Your Week

While I was writing this book, I was also planning my first women's event. In order to spend time with my family, meet my work objectives, and enjoy time with the Lord, I had to focus my time and attention on the things that would bear the most fruit.

In a perfect world, I would have liked a website completed before the event, but I didn't have the time or the skills. That had to take a back seat so that I could focus on more important things, like preparing the teaching for the event and sending out invitations. I could have spent hours trying to figure out how to create a website myself, but I chose to spend the time doing the things that God has gifted me in, teaching and organizing.

Sometimes we focus our efforts on things that we're not naturally good at doing instead of partnering with other people who excel in those areas. I didn't have time to track all of the invitations for the event or make the follow-up phone calls, so I partnered with someone who loves that kind of stuff. That person was instrumental in making sure that everyone invited felt loved and appreciated. Find people who love the things you loathe and give them the opportunity to participate in what you're doing by asking for their help.

> **Question:** Who do you know who loves tasks that you loathe? How might you be able to partner with that person to fulfill your God-given dreams?

_____

_____

_____

_____

_____

_____

Depending on your season of life, you may also need to adjust your expectations of how much you can accomplish. When I had my first child, my life changed more than I could have imagined. I didn't realize that my to-do list would look different during those first few months of staying home with my son.

After days of feeling frustrated, exhausted, and inadequate, I realized that I needed to adjust my expectations. My season had changed, which meant that my priorities had changed as well. I had to come to grips with the reality that, at that time, I couldn't pursue my

God-given dreams to the extent I would have liked.

That didn't mean I had to abandon my passions. Instead, I learned to be creative in how I worked toward my dreams and to enjoy the time I was able to spend with my son instead of getting frustrated that I wasn't checking as many things off my to-do list. I learned to set realistic goals and limit my to-do list to one or two things each day, at most.

You may feel like you don't have much time in this season of your life. If that's the case, I want you to identify one thing each week you can accomplish that would be significantly impactful. It may be organizing a room to make a workspace for yourself or a play space for your kids. It may be creating an account to start a blog or making a business start-up to-do list.

Pick just *one* step that is realistic. Then do everything in your power to make sure that you accomplish it. That accomplishment, even if it's small, will start to build momentum, and you will feel better about the direction your life is going. When we're not moving in any direction, we feel guilty, and that feeds more of our insecurities. When we know that we're taking small steps forward, it builds momentum, and momentum builds confidence.

Question: What is your one thing for the upcoming week?

_____

_____

_____

_____

_____

_____

Action Step Three: Realize You Don't Need Approval from Other People to Move Forward

In Galatians 1:10, Paul said, "Obviously, I'm not trying to win the approval of people, but of God. If pleasing people were my goal, I would not be Christ's servant" (NLT). While Paul made it clear who his master was, he also made it clear that he had to choose whose approval he was seeking. He knew whose approval was important and whose opinion he shouldn't value over God's.

All of us have the desire to please other people, and that's not a bad thing. However, we shouldn't allow the approval of others to become the guiding factor in our lives. We can't afford to let other people's opinions of us keep us from accomplishing the things that God has placed in our hearts.

There will always be doubters. There will always be people who don't understand our decisions. Don't allow them to stop you. If you are held captive by other people's opinions of you, you will live as a prisoner who has the keys to freedom in her hand.

Paul knew that he couldn't be Christ's servant while also being a people-pleaser. He had to choose one. Likewise, we won't become who God created us to be if we are hindered by a need for the approval of others.

This doesn't mean that we should stop loving people, serving them wholeheartedly, or even desiring to please them. It simply means that we shouldn't live our lives for their approval. Take off that heavy blanket of approval addiction and experience the freedom of becoming who God created you to be!

Sometimes (and I am guilty of this) we are so consumed with what other people might think of us that we don't allow the passion and love God has placed in our hearts to lead us. We're afraid of the social media likes we might not get, the engagement we might not have, or the followers we might lose instead of being afraid of missing out on the rich life we would have in following Jesus with all of our hearts and to the very best of our ability.

Question: Are you following God wholeheartedly, or are you seeking the approval of others? Does your concern over other people's opinions hold you back from God's calling on your life?

_____

_____

_____

_____

_____

_____

Question: What would your life look like if you were to stop allowing other people's opinions to dictate your actions? Take time to imagine just how different your life would be and how much freedom you would feel in your soul.

_____

_____

_____

_____

_____

_____

Action Step Four: Work as Though You're Working for the Lord

Colossians 3:23 tells us, "Whatever you do, work at it with all your heart, as working for the Lord, not for human masters" (NIV). I love to work, and I love working toward something I am passionate about. My character and my reputation are important to me. Because people know that I am a trustworthy and responsible person who will get the job done with excellence, I have developed great relationships in ministry and in the marketplace. My work ethic has helped to open many doors for me.

Think about the benefits of working hard for a good boss. You can earn a raise, a promotion, and awards and climb up the corporate ladder. When you work as though you are working for the Lord, the benefits are far greater than anything a human boss can give you. When you work as though you are working for the Lord, He will guide you to the right opportunities, and you will experience His power and provision in every area of your life.

I have personally experienced the fruit of a strong and determined work ethic. When I started my job, I was a minimum-wage employee with a college degree, making $8.00 per hour. But I never worked like a minimum-wage employee. I would get to work early, and I would stay late. I would offer solutions in a way that I knew they would be received. I worked as though the company were mine and put forth my full effort. I worked hard in toxic environments. I worked hard when I felt unseen and unheard. I worked hard and gave my best effort because I knew that it was the right thing to do.

Years later, I rose to the highest position in the company as President. I started at the very bottom and worked my way to the very top. You don't have to climb to the top of a company to prove that you're a hard worker. All I'm saying is that working with diligence and integrity opens doors. It builds resilience and grit. This is what happens when we work as though we are working for the Lord, even when no one else is watching us.

Developing an exceptional work ethic builds character in us that cannot be manufactured.

Wherever you are, work as though you're working for the Lord and allow the results to overwhelm you with goodness in due time. I'm not saying that you will have my story of blossoming beautifully. I'm saying that you will have your own story of blossoming beautifully.

Question: When you read Colossians 3:23, what comes to mind? What is one way you can begin living out this scripture today?

_____

_____

_____

_____

_____

_____

Action Step Five: Keep Hope Alive

It's easy to work exceptionally hard when we think that everything is going well. It's much more difficult to serve well when we're struggling with disappointment and discouragement. Do you remember how I shared in Chapter Four that I applied for the same administrative position three times? It didn't work out for me, and I was heartbroken.

Instead of giving into discouragement and disappointment, I moved on from my hurt feelings and kept plunging ahead at my current place of employment. About a year later, God gave me more favor in my job than I could have imagined. I also developed a great professional relationship with my CEO, and my love and passion for my job grew in the place where it was obvious that God had planted me.

Sometimes God is calling us to be faithful where we

are. A closed door is not always a rejection; it might be God's protection from something that's not meant for us, no matter how much we think we want it. Instead of calling us to move on, He may be looking to give us what we're looking for right where we are. Today, I can honestly say with all of my heart that I am thankful for the doors God closed. He opened doors for me that I didn't even know existed. When doors are closing, keep hope alive. Don't let discouragement and disappointment distract you from giving your all where God has you right now. Just an ounce of hope and a mustard seed of faith can go a long way!

> **Question:** Are you in a discouraging or disappointing situation? What steps can you take to keep hope alive and serve well where God has you right now?

_____

_____

_____

_____

_____

_____

Action Step Six: Be Vulnerable

Being vulnerable helps us to connect with others. There is a time and a place for this, and it's important to be wise when we're sharing our hearts with other people. With God, however, we can openly confess everything we are thinking and feeling. After all, He already knows!

I have been privileged to lead several teams, and there was a time when I thought that I had to know it all and do it all and be the best in order to be a good leader. I put on a facade with others and pretended that I was someone I wasn't, a know-it-all. Now I know better. I know the power in telling those who are under my leadership that I'm learning and failing forward. I see the value in asking people to be patient with me while I try to navigate through uncharted territory. I see the victory in sharing my struggles with those who are close to me instead of convincing myself that "I'm fine" during times when I'm struggling. I have seen first-hand the power in letting people in on your journey and the trust that is built with vulnerability.

Being appropriately vulnerable with other people helps to tear down the invisible wall we put up between ourselves and others. It reveals our humanity and shows us how much we all have in common. It takes courage to share our weaknesses and the areas of our lives where we are struggling. It's easier to pretend that we have it all together. But when we speak from our hearts, we speak to other people's hearts. People don't connect with our perfections as much as they connect with our pain and struggles.

I had a lesson in vulnerability when I was working with a career coach. She asked me to provide her with my bio. I worked on my bio for a few hours and submitted it. During our call, we went over my bio, and she told me that it didn't seem genuine. She was a bit surprised that I submitted something like that since I considered myself a writer. She could tell that I had included only what I wanted her to know.

Initially, I felt defensive and wanted to justify what I had written, but I didn't. I took heed and acknowledged the truth in what she said. After all, she was right. I didn't put much time into my bio, and I only shared what I felt others would want to hear. I didn't share from my heart. I held back instinctively, not intentionally. I thanked her for her feedback and went back to writing.

That week, I rewrote my bio. I really dug deep. There were moments when I felt tears forming as I wrote my story. During our next session, I also experienced her tears as I shared my new bio with her. I spoke from my heart, and I touched hers.

In that moment, I learned that vulnerability would need to be something that I intentionally bring into my life. I know now that it's the nitty-gritty things of the heart that truly connect with people. While I use wisdom and take some risks, there is freedom and connection when I choose vulnerability. Here's a snippet of the bio I wrote below. I want to share it with you to show you how the power of vulnerability played out in my life when I started the journey of this book by teaching its principles to a small classroom full of ladies:

> When I started teaching my class on fear, I found breakthrough. That was the moment in my life when I said, *"I'm exactly where I'm supposed to*

be." I was finding freedom in authenticity. Even though I could still control how close I allowed people to get to me and I had not yet found freedom in proximity to people, I was finding freedom through teaching the principles I was learning, principles that were changing my life. It was one of the most profound moments in my life—not because I left my fears, but because I stood in them without shame and I refused to allow them to control me. In this space, I not only unlocked my own chains, but I also had the key to unlock the chains of those around me. What made this experience so special was that I brought people into my space and into my pain and into my faith, and we all grew exponentially. I'll never forget that first class.

I challenge you not only to be real with God, but also to have the courage to be authentic with others. Let people know when you need a break, when you need help, or when you're having a bad day. Not everyone respects vulnerability, however, so be careful to exercise discernment regarding whom you share the intimate details of your heart with and how much you share. Value vulnerability and make it part of your life.

Question: Are there insecurities you're trying to secure by holding them inside and not sharing them with people you can trust? What would it look like for you to be more vulnerable with other people?

Love Well to Serve Well

There is one final trait that we need in order to serve well: love. It doesn't matter how well you apply the teaching in this chapter or how closely you follow the action plan if you're not placing love at the center of your service. If we serve based on love, we will consider other people before we talk and share our opinions. We will see that every single person we meet is battling something, and perhaps we would choose to forgive a lot quicker and not take things so personally. We choose to operate not in our emotions of the moment, but rather in steady, intentional love.

For me, serving out of love means doing the right thing even if it's not something I really want to do. For example, instead of sending an email full of assumptions, I'll ask questions. Instead of holding on to things that frustrate me, I'll pause and think through how to share my thoughts in a manner in which they will be well received. Instead of choosing suspicion, I'll choose to believe the best. Instead of holding on to resentment and pain, I'll surrender those things to God and ask Him to help me heal.

Putting love at the center of our service means choosing to forgive people who have hurt us and not holding resentment toward them. It means pressing through our pain and choosing to pray for and speak well of people who have wronged us. It's not easy, but it is liberating.

When we serve in love, we find healing, and love breaks through our pain and finds its way to the surface, where we experience freedom.

Love helps us to see Jesus in everyone. Love helps us to see Jesus through our pain. Love transforms our minds and our hearts. When we choose love, it leaps off the pages of the Bible, tears down walls, and breaks through barriers.

The Bible says that "knowledge puffs up while love builds up" (1 Corinthians 8:1 NIV). Love will build everything around you. Love will build your business. Love will build your passion. Love will build your relationships. Love will build your family and your friendships. Love will tear down walls and build bridges. It's the one thing we need for everything we want to build.

First Corinthians 13:1–3 (NLT) makes it clear that our spiritual gifts—in fact, all of our work and service—are useless without love:

If I could speak all the languages of earth and of angels, but didn't love others, I would only be a noisy gong or a clanging cymbal. If I had the gift of prophecy, and if I understood all of God's secret plans and possessed all knowledge, and if I had such faith that I could move mountains, but didn't love others, I would be nothing. If I gave everything I have to the poor and even sacrificed my body, I could boast about it; but if I didn't love others, I would have gained nothing.

So, what does love look like? First Corinthians 13:4–7 (NLT) continues:

Love is patient and kind. Love is not jealous or boastful or proud or rude. It does not demand its own way. It is not irritable, and it keeps no record of being wronged. It does not rejoice about injustice but rejoices whenever the truth wins out. Love never gives up, never loses faith, is always hopeful, and endures through every circumstance.

It doesn't matter what gifts we have if we do not have and share the gift of love. We will serve well if we seek to live a life of love. We can love well by showing empathy, compassion, and kindness, desiring the very best for others, not fixating on others' faults, and persevering with people through difficulties.

Get Set! Go!

In this chapter, we explored what it means to live for God with P.U.R.P.O.S.E. by serving others well:

1. Use the gifts God has given you. Serve bravely when you're faced with opposition. Instead of comparing yourself to others, know that every part of the body of Christ is important. Hold fast to the belief that your contribution matters!

2. Live a life of excellence. Celebrate others and suffer with them. Above all, love well!

3. Take action to serve from a healthy place of purpose. Work as though you're working for the Lord and bravely chase the dreams He has placed in your heart!

Serving well is a crucial part of living with P.U.R.P.O.S.E., and love is our guide to serving well. As we allow love to have its way and fuel our work and service, we will find ourselves thriving and not only moving toward our God-given dreams, but living the life of our dreams.

Chapter Eight Notes

Take some time to unpack all
your takeaways from this chapter

_____

_____

_____

_____

_____

_____

_____

_____

_____

_____

_____

_____

_____

_____

_____

_____

Enlist a Dream Team

If you think you're the entire picture, you will never see the big picture.[16]

—John Maxwell

Let me be totally honest with you: building a team hasn't always come naturally to me. I was more comfortable being an independent worker and working with people individually to accomplish a task. I love working with other people, but enlisting a dream team is outside of my comfort zone. I hate the thought of rejection and feeling like an inadequate leader. It's an area where I am continuing to grow and mature, but I'm going to tell you everything I have learned about building a dream team and being a part of God's community.

This chapter is all about investing in people, having fruitful relationships, and aligning yourself with people who are different from you. The projects I have undertaken and the things I have done as part of a team have been some of my most fruitful endeavors, even more so than some of the projects I have undertaken alone. *E* is the final letter in our P.U.R.P.O.S.E. acronym, and it stands for "Enlist a dream team."

Don't Just Invite People into Your Life; Invest in Their Lives

First things first. We need to know how to invite people into what we're doing. Jesus did it! If we truly desire a dream team, we need to have the courage to invite people into what we're doing and provide them with ways in which they can support us. Let me give you an example.

I have a friend who is launching a health and fitness business. I don't have a paid role in her business, but she leans on me for advice and encouragement. I am a part of her dream team, and my responsibility is simple: I believe in her, and I provide honest feedback and consistent encouragement. I am intentional about supporting her.

For some of us, it's important to assign people specific roles. We'll discuss that later in the chapter when we get to delegation, but first I want you to identify your support team. Who is in your corner, supporting you? Who is investing in you? From whom are you learning? You don't have to have someone managing your social media or becoming your administrative assistant. You can simply have people around you who help to keep you going in the right direction.

There's no way around it. We can certainly pray about having the right people on our team, and maybe God will have people fall into our laps and land in the right place.

But more often than not, we have to be willing to take action to create a dream team. We have to hand-select the people with whom to surround ourselves.

Sometimes creating a team requires us to ask for help personally and recruit people with specific skills. If you're paying someone, asking may not be as difficult, but if you're asking someone to help you but don't have a budget to pay that person, it can be a little intimidating. You know that you will have to be creative when it comes to compensation. I want to show you how you can confidently ask people to join you.

The first thing you need to do is determine how you're going to serve that person. It's all about recruiting with the right motives. In the words of John Maxwell, a well-known author in the field of leadership, "You are most valuable where you add the most value."[17] Jesus demonstrated the best and most unselfish approach when He called His disciples. His approach was not solely about Himself; it was about His disciples.

Let's take a look at how Jesus called Peter and Andrew to join Him:

As Jesus was walking beside the Sea of Galilee, he saw two brothers, Simon called Peter and his brother Andrew. They were casting a net into the lake, for they were fishermen. "Come, follow me," Jesus said, "and I will send you out to fish for people." At once they left their nets and followed him.
—Matthew 4:18–20 (NIV)

Jesus asked Peter and Andrew to leave everything they knew to follow Him. That was a pretty bold request! But He didn't just tell Peter and Andrew to follow Him. He gave them a vision of what their lives would look like if they chose to follow Him. Instead of being fishermen, they would become fishers of men.

Question: When you ask people to join you in your endeavors, do you identify your intention? How do you plan to serve them? What vision can you give them for the difference that joining you will make in their lives, their communities, and God's kingdom? How are you committed to their success?

_____

_____

_____

_____

_____

It's a lot more intimidating to ask someone to help us when it's solely for our benefit. When we invite people into something that will benefit them as well, it changes our motives. When our motive is the desire to help other people as well as ourselves, we're a lot less apprehensive and a lot more audacious.

When we have the desire to change someone's life for the better, we will be more eager and confident to invite people to partner with us. We will not fear rejection as much because we'll know with all of our hearts that we're giving them an opportunity, regardless of what we personally might gain.

How to Enlist Your Dream Team

Your time is valuable, and so is other people's. If you're going to invest your time in partnering with other people, it's important to find partners who have the character and work ethic you're looking for. You want to partner with people with qualities that will result in a good outcome for you and your team.

What qualities should we look for when investing in others, building a team, and developing partnerships? What type of leadership should we possess? What type of mentorship should we pursue? There's a passage in Exodus that gives us answers to these questions. Get ready because this section is packed with leadership goodness!

In chapter 18 of Exodus, Jethro, Moses's father-in-law, gave Moses some excellent advice that can benefit us as well. To give you some background, God called Moses to lead the Israelites out of slavery in Egypt and into the land that God had promised them. Jethro came to visit Moses while he was in the wilderness with the Israelites and observed everything Moses was doing for the people. He realized that Moses's approach to leadership wasn't as effective as it could be, and he offered his son-in-law some useful feedback:

The next day, Moses took his seat to hear the people's disputes against each other. They waited before him from morning till evening.

When Moses' father-in-law saw all that Moses was doing for the people, he asked, "What are you really accomplishing here? Why are you trying to do all this alone while everyone stands around you from morning till evening?"

Moses replied, "Because the people come to me to get a ruling from God. When a dispute arises, they come to me, and I am the one who settles the case between the quarreling parties. I inform the people of God's decrees and give them his instructions."

"This is not good!" Moses' father-in-law exclaimed. "You're going to wear yourself out—and the people, too. This job is too heavy a burden for you to handle all by yourself. Now listen to me, and let me give you a word of advice, and may God be with you. You should continue to be the people's representative before God, bringing their disputes to him. Teach them God's decrees, and give them his instructions. Show them how to conduct their lives. But select from all the people some capable, honest men who fear God and hate bribes. Appoint them as leaders over groups of one thousand, one hundred, fifty, and ten. They should always be available to solve the people's common disputes, but have them bring the major cases to you. Let the leaders decide the smaller matters themselves. They will help you carry the load, making the task easier for you. If you follow this advice, and if God commands you to do so, then

you will be able to endure the pressures, and all these people will go home in peace."

Moses listened to his father-in-law's advice and followed his suggestions. He chose capable men from all over Israel and appointed them as leaders over the people. He put them in charge of groups of one thousand, one hundred, fifty, and ten. These men were always available to solve the people's common disputes. They brought the major cases to Moses, but they took care of the smaller matters themselves.

—Exodus 18:13–26 (NLT)

Enlist a Mentor

Moses was a wise man. He didn't disregard instruction; he heeded it. He allowed someone with more wisdom to speak into his life and ministry, and he implemented the feedback. Likewise, it's important to have a mentor who has been where you're trying to go and can speak vision into what you're doing.

Jethro was obviously someone who had leadership skills. He knew something that Moses didn't know and saw things that Moses didn't see. Jethro had more knowledge and life experience than Moses had, and he helped to point Moses in the right direction. The first thing Jethro asked Moses to do was evaluate what he was doing versus what he was accomplishing.

A mentor will ask the right questions and help you to evaluate what you're doing.

A mentor will help you to consider how you're doing things and point you in the right direction.

I want to invite you to be someone who seeks out models from whom you can learn. More specifically, seek out people whose lives reflect God and His attributes. Find people who value other people, who have great integrity and a solid work ethic, and who are committed to growth in all areas of their lives.

As the saying goes, "Some things are caught, not taught." The most valuable lessons I have learned about life and character have come from watching other people. When my husband was a pastor, I met a man named Mickey Stonier. I attended Pastor Mickey's very first pastoral support team program. He stood in front of the class and quoted 1 Corinthians 8:1: "Knowledge puffs up while love builds up" (NIV).

He knew that the more knowledge we attained, the more we would be tempted to be prideful, and he wanted to help us nip that in the bud. I wanted to live out that scripture, and it soon became evident that Pastor Mickey was a person who did just that. He modeled what it looked like to use our knowledge to build others up with love rather than letting it puff us up with pride. Pastor Mickey was incredibly knowledgeable about the Bible and doctrine, yet he was also very humble. He had a way of living peaceably with everyone, even if some of their views were different from his.

As I began to serve in the church more, I realized how easy it was to argue about what the Bible says and what we believe as Christians. But Pastor Mickey inspired me to love people first instead of pushing my own views or engaging in pointless disputes with other believers.

Though he wasn't a personal mentor of mine, Pastor Mickey was certainly a model whom I intentionally watched. So look around you at work, in church, wherever you serve. Keep an eye out for people from whom you can learn. If you are looking for them, you will find them!

As your mentor right now, I want to ask you some questions similar to the ones Moses asked Jethro.

Question: Consider how your life is right now. What are you doing, and what are you really accomplishing? Identify the mentors and models in your life, the people you're watching, listening to, and learning from. How are they helping you to grow? Be specific. For example, instead of saying, "They are changing my perspective," you can say, "My mentor is helping me to see that I need to focus on how I am engaging in relationships. I have the tendency to withdraw when I'm scared. I didn't see that about myself before."

_____

_____

_____

_____

_____

_____

Jethro also gave Moses a warning. He saw something coming that Moses didn't see: burnout. Jethro warned Moses that continuing to lead in this way would wear him out. Moses's exhaustion would then trickle down to those who were under his leadership. This principle also applies to us. Taking on everything by ourselves is a recipe for burnout, and if we're leading other people, they, too, will experience the negative impact of our decisions to take on to much responsibility.

If you're trying to do everything all by yourself, let me be your "Jethro" for a second and tell you that you may be on the road to burning out. We all need someone. We all need help at some point. If you're not motivated, if you're tired and discouraged, evaluate how you're doing things and whether you're doing them alone. Then identify where you can use the most support and encouragement and simply ask for it. Ask for help from within your team or recruit someone onto your team.

A mentor will not deter you from your life work. A mentor will simply help you to do your life work better.

Jethro didn't say, "Stop what you're doing." He said, "You can do it more efficiently by selecting qualified people to whom you can delegate."

If you're looking for a mentor and perhaps are discouraged because you don't have one or have never had one, it's important that you do some digging and figure out exactly what you want out of a mentoring relationship. Saying something like, "I want to grow spiritually," isn't specific enough. You need to ask yourself what growing spiritually would look like in your life. Does it mean that you want to learn how to study the Bible? Does it mean that you want to start teaching other people? Decide what you want your specific outcome to be.

Second, as a mentee, know that it's okay to have different types of mentors. Some mentors might speak into your spiritual life, and some mentors might speak into your professional life. You can have many different types of mentors and models. Some mentors are not with you for a lifetime; they are for a moment in time. Jesus was only with His disciples for three years. When you have the opportunity to get mentored, take full advantage of it.

Determine what areas of your life you want to grow in and find people who are thriving in those areas. Then take that step of faith and ask if they would be willing to mentor you or speak into what you're doing.

Question: How do you plan to build a mentoring relationship?

_____

_____

_____

_____

_____

_____

Question: How specifically do you want to grow? Identify at least one thing you can do to move yourself in the direction of growth.

_____

_____

_____

_____

_____

_____

Question: What's your next step to having mentorship in your life?

_____

_____

_____

_____

_____

_____

A mentor should get involved in the life of his or her mentee, and a mentee should give the mentor access to his or her life. Moses gave Jethro access to his life and permission to speak into his ministry. As the mentor, Jethro provided wise counsel and insight regarding how Moses could lead more effectively and sustainably.

If you desire to mentor, help your mentees to figure out what they want and how they want to grow. If you both know what you're aiming for, it will make your time that much more fruitful.

When you enlist a dream team, look for someone you can pour into and help to grow. This isn't something you need to manufacture; this is a relationship that should come naturally. Just as Jesus chose His twelve closest disciples, choose the people you want to invest in, bring them into your life, and teach them what you know and what you're learning.

Enlist with Intention

Leading is probably one of the most challenging positions. It's the position that carries the most weight and the most responsibility. I used to think that leading was sitting around, giving orders, but it's not. Leading is constant growth on your part, hard decisions, hard conversations, and a full commitment to learning. As you lead your life, your family, and your passion, I can assure you that it will require you to lead yourself and other people in some capacity. Leadership can be simple and complicated all at the same time, but Jethro gave us some advice we can keep close to heart and apply to our lives.

1. Jethro told Moses, "Do what you can do." There are some things that you are gifted and equipped to do well.

These are the roles and tasks that you can and should do. You need to identify those things and then delegate the rest to others. In my work, I am the one person who can give insight regarding the direction we're going. My role is the visionary. That doesn't mean I don't get input on where I'm taking things. It just means that I am the ultimate decision maker when it comes to the direction of our team.

In my ministry life, no one can write my book or my teachings. These are things I have to and should focus on. If I am focused on things that other people can do, then I'm probably not investing enough time in the tasks only I can do. Start with the things only you can do. You can make a plan, create action steps, do the things you're already good at doing, and lead other people in the right direction. If you're overwhelmed with several ideas, just pick one and start with that. You don't have to start all of them at once. Ask yourself, *"What can I do?"*

2. Jethro said, "Teach the people." Leadership is all about helping people to learn. You have a responsibility to make sure that you're equipping your team. A teacher can help to challenge and change your way of thinking. A teacher empowers you. A teacher is also a student. When you're responsible for teaching others, your learning never stops. How are you teaching those around you to be better? How are you adding value to their lives and helping them to grow? If you want to be a good leader, you need to commit yourself to learning constantly and developing those around you.

3. Jethro said, "Give instructions." Giving instructions is the launching pad to a thriving endeavor. People need clear direction. If we don't give clear instructions, we're setting people up for failure. We have to be willing to teach or show people how things are accomplished. In order to give good instructions, we need to be able to communicate clearly. This is an art. As the leader, you're responsible for ensuring that the people to whom you're giving instructions understand the outcome you desire. This means that you first need to know exactly what you want.

When people don't do something the way we want, it may not be their fault. Our communication may be to blame. We need to make sure that our instructions are clear and everyone on the receiving end fully understands them. Clear communication begins with clarity of thought and requires knowing the people on your team. Know what you want and think through exactly how to communicate it in a way that ensures your message is received accurately.

4. Jethro described to Moses the type of people whom he should select to be part of his leadership team. There are qualities we should look for when building partnerships and finding people to work alongside us. We need to ask ourselves, *"Are they capable?"* Do they have the skills and willingness to complete the task well? They can't just be kind; they need to be capable.

Are they honest? You can only trust people who are honest. You may not always like what they have to say, but you will benefit from their honesty. Honesty is trust-building, and you can build with someone you trust.

Are they God-fearing? Is doing the right thing, including living by godly standards, important to them? Do they have a personal relationship with God? Are they people of integrity? We need to look at how they live and how they treat people around them. Not everyone we partner with will have a relationship with Jesus, but it's important to know if someone is a person of integrity before we invite that person onto our team.

Are they reputable? If you can see that they have a moral compass that guides their life, you can trust that a bribe won't tickle their ears. As a leader, I have made some mistakes by recruiting competency over integrity, and it cost me a lot when everything was said and done. Now I know better, and I watch for character. I listen for it in conversations. I look for it in a person's work ethic. When enlisting a dream team, these are essential qualities to consider.

5. *Appoint leaders and delegate according to what they can handle.* When we see people thriving in their positions, we often assume that they can handle more. Then, once they have more responsibility, we may notice that they're not as efficient. It's important to know not only whom you want, but also how much each person can handle well. Moses appointed some men over a thousand, some over one hundred, some over fifty, and some over ten. An overwhelmed leader is less efficient and less creative.

Make sure that the people to whom you're delegating work have the capacity to accomplish what you're asking.

I partner with professionals to accomplish tasks for my ministry. They help me with things like video and photography. When someone is too busy to call me back or answer my emails, that's an indication to me that I'm working with someone who may not have the capacity to accomplish what I'm requesting. Punctuality, organization, consistent communication, and attentiveness are the things I look for when I'm delegating a project. Lack of effectiveness, creativity, compassion, and enthusiasm are things I see when I'm working with people who may have more on their plates than they can handle.

As a leader, delegate the things you can't do and the things that keep you away from what you're supposed to be doing. Jethro made it clear that the people Moses chose would help him to carry the load of leadership. Ask yourself what areas are weighing you down. If those tasks are necessary, enlist people to help you carry the load.

6. *Finally, be coachable.* The Bible says, "Moses listened to his father-in-law's advice and followed his suggestions" (Exodus 18:24 NLT). Moses listened, and he followed. Listening to advice and implementing suggestions are key components of good leadership. We need to open our ears to wise advice and be humble and disciplined enough to implement the things we believe will help us to serve people better and accomplish our mission. I remember a mentor telling me that I should use a communication tool called Slack App because it worked so well for that person's team and project management. I tried using it but quickly found that it wasn't a tool that

could easily be woven into the culture of our organization. I had to figure out something else that would work better.

When you try to implement the advice of someone you trust, it may not always work for your team and situation. That's part of the process of being a student and a professional learner in the service of others.

> **Behind anyone who has accomplished something great, you'll find a whisper, a loud voice, an advocate, or a coach in the shadows who helped that person to get there.**

Seek Good Friends

Lastly, we need friends on our dream team. This may be one person, or it may be several. When God called Moses to lead the Israelites out of Egypt, he was afraid and felt inadequate, especially when it came to public speaking (Exodus 4:10). God provided Aaron to come alongside Moses and do what Moses wasn't able to do at that time:

> *"All right," he [the LORD] said. "What about your brother, Aaron the Levite? I know he speaks well. And look! He is on his way to meet you now. He will be delighted to see you. Talk to him, and put the words in his mouth. I will be with both of you as you speak, and I will instruct you both in what to do. Aaron will be your spokesman to the people.*

*He will be your mouthpiece, and you will stand in
the place of God for him, telling him what to say."*
— **Exodus 4:14–16 (NLT)**

Aaron filled in that gap for Moses and helped him to
be who God created him to be. Maybe you're like Moses
and you recognize that God has given you someone who
will come alongside you like Aaron did for Moses. Or
maybe you're like Aaron, the friend who comes alongside
someone else to fill in the gaps.

Question: What friend(s) has God placed in your
life to come alongside you? What type of friend do
you desire to be to someone else?

_____

_____

_____

_____

_____

_____

It's easy to be intimidated by and jealous of people who
are going places we desire to go. We need to fight against
the temptation to compare ourselves to others and choose
instead to be a good friend to someone we love. We need
to be willing to step into the gap and be what others cannot
be for themselves at that moment. Friendships take time
and require us to be vulnerable. Some friendships show us

the messy parts of our hearts that we need to acknowledge and choose to change. We need to be willing to risk our hearts and be intentional about pursuing relationships if we want to experience rich friendships.

Proverbs 18:24 says, "One who has unreliable friends soon comes to ruin, but there is a friend who sticks closer than a brother" (NIV). I can't help but feel hopeful knowing that God has a friend for me who sticks closer than a brother, and I also want to be that friend for someone else. You might have been hurt by a friend and experienced heartache from someone you trusted, but there is still hope for you. Start by being the friend you want to find and believe that God has a friend for you who will stick closer than a brother.

Question: Take a moment to consider what you have learned in this chapter about enlisting a team. What is one practical step you can take in your personal or professional life that will bring you closer to having a dream team?

_____

_____

_____

_____

_____

Get Set! Go!

In this chapter, we discussed keys to enlisting a dream team in the course of pursuing your life of P.U.R.P.O.S.E.:

1. Invest in other people's lives.

2. Look around you for people with wisdom and experience you can learn from. Good leadership requires you to learn continually.

3. Look for key characteristics in the people you invite onto your team. Make sure that they are capable, hard-working people of integrity. Learn how to communicate with your team members clearly and effectively.

4. Be a trustworthy, supportive friend and seek good friends.

To enlist a dream team, we have to value people and their potential. We have to see the best and believe the best in other people and also in ourselves. Pursuing and cultivating relationships and community is key not only in living out our God-given dreams, but also in living a rich and fruitful life with Jesus. We need to have people in our corner, business partners who complement us, leaders who come alongside us, team members who work with us, mentors who help us to navigate uncharted territory, and friends who encourage us along the way. Choose your dream team wisely. These are the people you will serve and the people who will fill in the gaps for you as you continue to live on P.U.R.P.O.S.E.

If you already have a team, keep pressing forward and applying what you have learned. If you're starting from scratch, go build! You've got this!

Chapter Nine Notes

*Take some time to unpack all
your takeaways from this chapter*

_____

_____

_____

_____

_____

_____

_____

_____

_____

_____

_____

_____

_____

_____

_____

_____

_____

Rise

Living with P.U.R.P.O.S.E. isn't a destination; it's your personal journey with Jesus, a lifelong adventure continuously unfolding. It's full of highs, lows, and unexpected detours. I have found through personal experience and research that so much of what we discover in life has to do with facing the truth about ourselves and being courageous enough to do our own life work. This book was about your journey, and congrats to you because you decided before you even began reading this book that growth is possible and your life should be purposeful.

Every chapter of this book was designed with you in mind. Each chapter has tools to help you evaluate your current situation and make the next best choice to move in the direction of your purpose. The P.U.R.P.O.S.E. principles are meant to help you fully engage with Jesus and others as you live life on purpose. This isn't a one-time read. It's designed to be helpful every time you need clarity and direction in any area of your life. Come back to these chapters when you feel stuck. They will help you to take action and move forward in the right direction.

God will give you many dreams and passions over the course of your life, and they will turn out in different ways. Some may meet your expectations, and others may not. But it's the same God who gives all of these dreams, and we can trust His purposes.

Fulfilling a God-given dream doesn't mean that you will reach everyone, but you will reach someone.

No matter the number of people you reach, your effort is marked in eternity. Pursue what God has placed in your heart and leave the results to Him. Take a moment to envision who might benefit from your dream becoming a reality, the people who might be helped, healed, or encouraged. As you step out in obedience and pursue the things that God places in your heart, you will inspire other people to do the same.

Living on P.U.R.P.O.S.E. isn't easy. It requires commitment, sacrifice, and perseverance in the face of obstacles. It requires faith in God's ability to lead you, especially when you're unsure of your destination or how you're going to get there. Becoming the person God created you to be will require you to face your fears and step out in faith, even when other people don't understand.

There will be times when you are tempted to give up and return to your old way of doing things. Don't resort to a life you'll regret, a life of simply getting by. The easy, comfortable way isn't worth it. You only have one life on this earth, so make it an adventure!

God has called you to live an amazing life beyond what you can imagine, so open yourself up to it! Don't let fear keep you from thriving. You have come too far to quit, so don't give up now. Keep leaning into Jesus and pressing forward into all that He has in store for you. Hold on to hope with all of your might. No matter what happens, know that God's got you. Never stop believing in who God is and what He has placed in your heart.

Consider me the coach in your corner, cheering you on. You can do this, girl! Rise!

Seven-Day Solitude Plan

Find a peaceful place where you can spend at least ten minutes with Jesus. The activity may take more than ten minutes, and that's okay. Do what you can and modify the plan as needed. This is not a formula for spending time with the Lord; it's a simple method that can help you to get started.

1) Read the day's scripture and take time to meditate on it. If you can memorize it, great!

2) Take time to journal about one or more of the following prompts:

   a. What are some words or phrases that really stand out to you? Why?

   b. What does this scripture communicate about God's heart for you personally and for all of humankind?

    c. What does this scripture communicate about God and His character, attributes, love, and promises?

    d. How would believing and living out this scripture radically change your life? What would it feel like to experience the fruit of this scripture in your life?

    e. How can you apply this scripture to your everyday life?

3) Pray to the Lord using the T.R.A.A.C.T.S. acronym:

    a. Thank Him and praise Him.

    b. Repent and confess.

    c. Acknowledge Him in every area of your life. Consider your roles as a spouse, parent, friend, and business professional. Think about what God has done for you in the past, what He is doing in your life right now, and what you believe He can do for you in the future.

    d. Ask God for what you want.

    e. Consider those around you and closest to you, such as family and friends. This is the time when I want you to consider other people and things outside of yourself and pray for them.

f. Take time to listen to what God is saying to you.

g. Say "thank You" again.

Here is the list of Bible verses for you to meditate on each day:

Day One: "Let the morning bring me word of your unfailing love, for I have put my trust in you. Show me the way I should go, for to you I entrust my life" (Psalm 143:8 NIV).

Day Two: "Trust in the LORD with all your heart and lean not on your own understanding; in all your ways submit to him, and he will make your paths straight" (Proverbs 3:5–6 NIV).

Day Three: "My frame was not hidden from you when I was made in the secret place, when I was woven together in the depths of the earth. Your eyes saw my unformed body; all the days ordained for me were written in your book before one of them came to be" (Psalm 139:15–16 NIV).

Day Four: "Rejoice always, pray without ceasing, give thanks in all circumstances; for this is the will of God in Christ Jesus for you" (1 Thessalonians 5:16–18 ESV).

Day Five: "For God so loved the world that he gave his one and only Son, that whoever believes in him shall not perish but have eternal life" (John 3:16 NIV).

Day Six: "I am writing to you who are God's children because your sins have been forgiven through Jesus" (1 John 2:12 NLT).

Day Seven: "The LORD says, 'I will guide you along the best pathway for your life. I will advise you and watch over you'" (Psalm 32:8 NLT).

I pray that the Seven-Day Solitude Plan will help you as you begin spending time in God's Word. May you pursue God continually on your journey of living on P.U.R.P.O.S.E.!

About the Author

When I started teaching my class on the P.U.R.P.O.S.E. principles found in this book, I experienced a lot of breakthrough and it was the moment in my life when I said, I'm exactly where I'm supposed to be, I found the thing I was made for! I was finding freedom through teaching the principles I was not only learning but the principles that were changing my life. I knew with all my heart that I had to press through my fears if I wanted to live with purpose. Teaching my class on the very thing I was living out at the time was one of the most profound moments in my life. Not because I left my fears but because I stood in them without shame, and I refused to allow them to control me. What made this experience so special, is that I brought people into my space and into my pain and into my faith and we all grew – exponentially. And now, I am bringing you into the same space. This book isn't just teaching points, this book is my story of pressing through and forging forward. I know what it's like to be paralyzed by fear and limiting beliefs and I know what it's like to sit in the shadows when I know in my heart I was made to shine. For every woman who can relate, I wrote this book for you. I have done a lot of work to transform some of my greatest fears into power and purpose and I feel compelled to give back what was given to me.

I give women tools to help them lean into their passion, press through their fears, and build a life they love.

REFERENCES

Notes

1. *Blue Letter Bible,* "Strong's G3404 – *miseōI.*" https://www.blueletterbible.org/lang/lexicon/lexicon.cfm?Strongs=G3404&t=KJV.

2. Forleo, Marie. *Everything Is Figureoutable.* Publishing Group, 2020.

3. Maxwell, John C. *Motivated to Succeed.* Grupo Nelson, 2006.

4. Bible in One Year (app). "January 12 Day 12: No Fear." https://bibleinoneyear.org/bioy/commentary/3919.

5. Hollis, Rachel. "My Morning Routine." Rachel Hollis (website). April 3, 2019. https://msrachelhollis.com/2019/04/03/.

6. Angelou, Maya. *And Still I Rise: A Book of Poems.* Random House Publishing Group, 2011.

7. Ellicott, Charles J. *A Bible Commentary for English Readers.* Vol. 6, *The Four Gospels.* Cassell and Company,

1905.

8. *Blue Letter Bible,* "Strong's G964 – *bēthesda.*" https://www.blueletterbible.org/lang/lexicon/lexicon.cfm?Strongs=G964&t=KJV.

9. Bible Study. "Meaning of Numbers in the Bible: The Number 5." https://www.biblestudy.org/bibleref/meaning-of-numbers-in-bible/5.html.

10. Ellicott, Charles J. *A Bible Commentary for English Readers.* Vol. 6, *The Four Gospels.* Cassell and Company, 1905.

11. Cook, Amanda. "Heroes," track 1 on *Brave New World.* Bethel Music, September 25, 2015.

12. *Online Etymology Dictionary,* "dis-." https://www.etymonline.com/word/Dis-.

13. *Lexico,* "discouragement." https://www.lexico.com/synonyms/discouragement.

14. Bible Study. "Meaning of Numbers in the Bible: The Number 12." https://www.biblestudy.org/bibleref/meaning-of-numbers-in-bible/12.html.

15. Abayilo, Lami. *Supreme Secrets of Success.* Salem Author Services, 2010, p. 120.

16. Maxwell, John C. *Team: The 17 Indisputable Laws of Teamwork: Winning with People.* Thomas Nelson, 2008, p. 21.

17. Maxwell, *Team,* p. 44.

www.ingramcontent.com/pod-product-compliance
Lightning Source LLC
LaVergne TN
LVHW052018080426
835513LV00018B/2076